WANTREPRENEUR

TO

ENTREPRENEUR

Wantrepreneur

to

Entrepreneur

What You Really Need to Know to Start Your First Business

Brian Lofrumento

Dawn –
Anything is possible!

BL

Wantrepreneur to Entrepreneur

What You Really Need to Know to Start Your First Business

First printing, 2015

ISBN 13: 978-1519281111

ISBN 10: 1519281110

Books may be purchased in quantity by contacting the author, Brian Lofrumento, by email at hello@imetbrian.com

To request a speaking engagement, contact the author at hello@imetbrian.com

Dedication

To my mom and dad (Lina and Paul), who have always made me feel like there are no limits to what I can accomplish and who have instilled a sense of hard-work and gratitude in my life… none of this would have been possible without you both

To my brother and sister (Michael and Kristina), who have taught me many of my most important life lessons, and who have always been my most reliable friends in the world

To my Uncle Fron, who inspired me to always want to be a writer "when I grow up"

To Zain, who is the only person I've ever met that can match my tireless work ethic around the clock, and for helping me grow Premiership Talk beyond our wildest dreams

Table of Contents

If you want to get an entrepreneur excited, ask him or her about the very first dollar they made as an entrepreneur. In that very moment – no matter what the dollar amount is – you go from being a "wantrepreneur" (or someone who wants to be an entrepreneur) to an entrepreneur.

Trust me... every entrepreneur remembers their first dollar. No matter how many companies you start, the first deal in each one always feels like the best one.

Back in 2008 when I started my first "real" business at the age of 19, I was on top of the world when Premiership Talk, my soccer website, made its first dollar. In hindsight it's funny to look back on, because it was a measly $200 for an entire month of advertising, but I will never forget the company who bought the advertising space, the owner's name who reached out to me, and what their banner ad looked like.

The thing is... that $200 deal gave me all the confidence in the world, and set me up for every dollar I've made since then.

Most recently, in 2014 I decided to take all of my knowledge of creating automated, scalable marketing systems and package it into a four week online workshop called the **4 Weeks to a Profitable Funnel Workshop**. I had no clue if anyone would buy it, but everyone was constantly asking me if I could teach them what I know, so I decided to put it out into the world and see if anyone would buy it. After I launched it by listing it for sale on an industry forum, I went to bed.

Every night before I fall asleep, I can't help but check my phone one last time (you know... just in case anything exciting happened in the three minutes between me turning off the computer and getting into bed).

That particular night – June 15th, 2014 – I had an email from PayPal. "You've got money!" read the subject line.

Words can't properly express my joy at seeing those words, and opening up the email to realize that I had been paid $197 from a stranger in Romania. There might not be a better feeling in the world than your first deal.

So why am I telling you this? Because if you're reading this book, then chances are you're a wantrepreneur, or a very beginner-stage entrepreneur who still struggles with growing a business, and most possibly is still stuck in the wantrepreneur mindset.

And I've got news for you... you're in store for the most exciting part of your life.

The reason I've written this book is because *I love wantrepreneurs*. Every great entrepreneur was once a wantrepreneur who decided to smash through all of the reasons why society said they "couldn't do" something. Every great entrepreneur was once a wantrepreneur who decided to take their life into their own hands and live life on their own terms. And most importantly, every great entrepreneur was once a wantrepreneur who was terrified of the journey, yet still jumped off the cliff, trusting that they could build a plane on the way down.

In 1932 Amelia Earhart etched her name into history by becoming the first ever solo female to fly nonstop over the Atlantic Ocean. She endured a nearly 15 hour flight from Newfoundland, Canada all the way to Culmore in Northern Ireland despite strong winds, icy conditions, and mechanical problems.

Written on the side of her plane was the phrase "Always think with your stick forward." From an aviation perspective, Amelia was clearly pointing out that if you slow down then you'll crash, but her message offers profound insights into what it means to be an entrepreneur.

Starting a business, just like flying across the Atlantic Ocean, is a scary and monumental task. But just like in aviation, you must think with your stick forward. All too often we choose not to act, not to move forward. We do this for plenty of reasons: because we're scared, because people tell us we can't do it, because we "don't have the time," or because we can just do it tomorrow.

In this book, I'll share with you all of the things that I learned as I was flying with my accelerator stick in the forward position. It's the times when I was moving forward faster than I was ready for that I learned the most, and that alone has enabled me to grow multiple six-figure businesses, have my website reach over 3.5 million people from over 200 countries around the world, and work with over 3,000 students from around the world.

1

The Key Ingredient of All Successful Endeavours: Starting!

"The longer you wait for the future the shorter it will be."

It's only appropriate that a book about going from wantrepreneur to entrepreneur starts with... well... **starting!** If there's one way to guarantee that you'll never become an entrepreneur, it's to not start. Starting is, without a doubt, the single most defining moment in any adventure or journey we embark on.

The good news about starting is that it's easy. Think about starting a diet. Let's pretend you want to change your diet to not eat red meat anymore. Even if you're the world's biggest red meat lover, starting this diet is no problem at all... go a day without eating red meat, and you've successfully started – and completed! – one day of your new diet.

This may sound like a simplistic example, but it's really no surprise that starting anything is easy. The same scenario can apply to starting a new exercise regime. Let's say that you want to commit to a new exercise plan of running one mile every day. Go outside, run one mile, and BOOM! You've done it again! You've successfully **started** something new!

Of course, you and I both know that sustaining any new project, program, or commitment is the really hard part. From the above examples, we both know it's not hard to start.

Start Every Day

Seth Godin discusses the concept of starting in his book *Poke the Box*. He uses the example of walking to Cleveland. In his example, he invites you to pretend that you're walking to Cleveland. From where I live (Boston), that would be a 600 mile walk. If I were to embark on this journey, starting would be easy... I'd walk outside, and start heading west. One mile in, I could safely say that I started walking to Cleveland.

In *Poke the Box*, Seth Godin points out that after a day of walking (let's say you're 20 miles closer to Cleveland at the end of day one), one of two things can happen the next morning: you can quit, or you can start again. Seth argues that every step is a new beginning, and I'm inclined to agree.

When starting a business, your energy is likely at the highest it's ever been. The excitement of newpreneurs is infectious, and it's a core reason why I enjoy interacting with and helping them so much. At the beginning, everything is new, opportunities are abundant, and the direction is pretty much unknown... a million things could possibly happen, all leading to very different outcomes!

The challenge when starting is to start again, each and every day. While the beginning is the easiest part, it's also the hardest part. You don't have any processes at the beginning, nor do you have any customers or clients. Which, perhaps most importantly for you if you don't have a safety net of savings, means that there's no money coming in. That's hard.

So having the mindset of starting every day is essential. I don't know anyone who hates distance running more than I do, so this concept is particularly useful to me. When going for a five mile run, I mentally need to "start" again every single lap. At the end of each lap around the track, I have a choice to make: I can quit right then and there and never make it to five miles, or I can start again with another lap. If I'm serious about running the five miles, then more often than not, I choose the latter, and the same needs to be true when you start your business.

I've never been a smoker, but growing up both of my parents were. As I entered my teenage years and society became more aware of the impacts of second-hand smoke, both of my parents decided to quit smoking. So, they went one day without smoking.

Then, the next day, they had a decision: they could start again by going one more day without smoking, or they could quit the initiative and just light up again.

Luckily, both of them went cold turkey. They sustained their initiative, but only by starting every day. Every single day they had to decide to not smoke, until it became natural.

In your business, you need to start every day. Particularly at the beginning when you're looking for your first client, you need to start again every day. Go to networking events, reach out to people, knock on doors, make some phone calls, send some emails. And if it doesn't work… start again tomorrow. Of course, you need to be wise about not always trying the same thing and expecting different results, but the point is that you need to view each day as a decision point in your journey: are you going to go on, or call it quits? It's one or the other.

Starting Before You're Ready

Over the years I've been fortunate enough to interact with entrepreneurs at all different stages of business, and across all different industries. I've hung out with entrepreneurs who make $40k per year, entrepreneurs who make $500k per month, and entrepreneurs whose businesses now do over $30 million per year.

The one constant between all of them is that they all say they wish they started sooner.

Whenever I speak to large groups of wantrepreneurs or business students, inevitably someone in the crowd always asks what advice I would give them.

My answer is always the same... start before you're ready. I was fortunate enough to not even realize what I was doing when I started my first online business, Premiership Talk. I started it completely out of boredom, and at 3am I spontaneously decided that I wanted to own a soccer blog.

I had no clue what I was doing, I had no experience in creating a blog, and I had absolutely zero experience in growing a blog's traffic. But, at 19 years old, I didn't know any better, so I plowed forward.

Sure enough, when you just start, you quickly realize that everything is figure out-able.

My first challenge was to figure out how to actually create a blog and get it live on the internet. Then, I had to figure out how to buy and setup a domain name (for a while the site operated as premtalk.blogger.com rather than premiershiptalk.com). Then, I had to figure out how to format the blog's look and feel to my satisfaction. Part of that meant I had to become somewhat competent with regards to graphic design. Then I had to figure out how to best write a blog post (in terms of length, voice, etc.). Then I had to figure out how to get traffic. Fast forward a few months and I had to figure out how to sell advertising space and make money from the site.

Wow! The challenges seriously never ended. But... because I had started, I just took each challenge as they came. One at a time. Everything was figure out-able.

Meanwhile, I'm sure there was someone else out there in the world that also wanted to start a soccer blog, but decided they wanted to wait until they were ready and had solutions for the above challenges I mentioned. Chances are that person never felt "ready" enough to start, because in the end you're never "ready."

Nine months into my Premiership Talk journey, I *really* learned what it meant to start before I was ready. At 20 years of age, I got my first big break with Prem Talk. A reader from England who worked in a soccer shop saw a picture of the new – and unreleased but much anticipated – England national team jersey. This reader emailed me a picture from his phone, and I ran with that story, having gotten my hands on that picture before any other website.

Traffic exploded that day, with tens of thousands of readers flooding in (which was a **huge** increase on the hundreds of readers I typically had on a daily basis at that time).

The next day, though, something I wasn't "ready" for happened, and I thought it would bring me crashing down. A major company involved in the manufacturing of the jersey was not at all pleased that I published images before they officially released the jersey to the world, and had already gotten their legal department involved.

"Legal department!?" I gasped. Here they were with an entire legal department, and I was a 20-year-old blogger in a dorm room. I certainly wasn't ready for the legal battle, but I figured it out. In the end, I rallied my website's fans and readers together, and stood my ground. That in turn got the website even more attention from bigger media websites, and in the long-run was a key contributor to getting Premiership Talk on the map.

If I had waited until I was ready for an encounter like that, I'd still be waiting today. I still don't have a "legal department" to fight a situation like that, and I'm not sure I ever will. But millions of readers and thousands of advertising dollars later, I sure am glad that I started before I was ready!

Everything is figure out-able.

Be Naïve

Along the same lines as starting before you're ready, at the beginning you need to understand that it's okay to be naïve.

It's okay to start and have no idea where your company will end up. So many times we're taught that we need to know our direction before we get going, when in fact **any** progress will take us beyond where we stand today.

Naivety can be a huge advantage when it comes to entrepreneurship. I was fortunate to naturally be naïve when I got started due to my age, but regardless of age you can use naïveté to your advantage.

If I had understood the task at hand when I started Premiership Talk, there's no way I would have started. If I had set out determined to make Premiership Talk the most-read soccer website in the world, it would have never reached the heights that it did. Naivety meant that I started without knowing where I was going, which meant that I was never paralyzed with fear regarding the monumental task in front of me.

Somewhere in the world, someone was sitting at a computer and decided that there was no way they could go from zero to over a million readers per month. And you know what? They were right. It's crazy to think that you could do that. One might say you have to be **naïve** to believe that you could do it.

And that's precisely what I was. If I set out targeting a million readers per month, there's no way I would have trudged through the many months of only getting hundreds of readers. But instead, I started afresh every day. Soon enough my hundreds of readers became a thousand. And a thousand became ten thousand per month. And soon enough that became 100,000 readers per month. And after years of work, Premiership Talk became one of the most-read soccer websites in the world, to the point where we were named the FA Cup Fans' Favorite Football (soccer) Site by the English Football Association.

...had I not been naïve, and had I set out with all of those goals in my head from the outset, I would have been paralyzed.

It's okay to just start. Any progress is progress. Even small progress compounded over months and years can change the world.

Asking for Help and Advice

All of our lives we've been told to ask for help when we need it. Ever since we were kids in school, we were told to ask others for advice.

There's definitely a time and a place for that. By no means do I think that we as entrepreneurs or as humans should stand alone as islands, but I've seen too many wantrepreneurs remain waiting in the wings after asking people for advice.

Before we go any further, understand that asking for advice and help is smart in certain circumstances. In fact, I've saved myself many headaches and disasters by asking for advice from people who have gone through different experiences.

But, at the beginning, be wary about the advice that other people can give you. At the start you have absolutely nothing to lose, so limit the amount of advice that you solicit from others.

I've always been a fan of "guided discovery," where people learn on their own from their own experiences, but can always have someone guiding them towards making the right decisions. The key in this approach is to never **tell** people the answer; within guided discovery the only goal of the teacher is to create an environment conducive to the students learning through their own experiences, successes, and failures.

New entrepreneurs (newpreneurs) have the habit of asking everyone around them for advice. Too often, very few people around us are entrepreneurs (a trend which will hopefully change!).

If you're a wantrepreneur or a newpreneur and you ask non-entrepreneurs (I suppose I could say nonpreneurs!) for advice, then take it with a grain of salt. After all, they've never **experienced** entrepreneurship, so they're speaking from a point of speculation.

I've also seen people offer advice as a third-party witness. For example, I've lost count of the number of times people have told me "oh, I know someone who started a blog, but there's no money in that."

Sorry, but a) I don't know who you know, but they don't work as hard or as smart as I do, and b) you really don't know what they've done – or not done – to get the results (or lack of results) that they've gotten.

Even if you think you're asking the "right" person for advice because they've accomplished exactly what you hope to accomplish, it may not be the best approach. No two journeys are **ever** the same, especially in business. If we could clone Mark Zuckerberg today and put the clone back at Harvard and make him take the exact same steps that the real life Mark Zuckerberg took as he was growing Facebook, there's no way the cloned Facebook would enjoy the same rapid rate of growth. There are too many moving parts, and the world changes every second.

I could tell you every little detail about how I grew my soccer blog into a full-fledged business with a writing staff of 20 people, but there's no guarantee it would work for you. In fact, none of my advice may be pertinent to you, because today is a new day.

I always laugh when I see people asking for other people's opinions and letting those opinions sway their own decision-making process. The most classic example I see is when people ask how they should go about getting their first client or customer.

Before I even know what advice you're given, I can already tell what the advice will be based on who you decide to ask. For example, if you ask an internet marketer how you should get your first customer or client, they'll tell you to create a website and drive traffic to that website. If you ask a social media expert, they'll tell you to use social media. If you ask your 90-year-old grandfather, he'll tell you to buy a newspaper ad.

When you ask people for advice, you're already selecting what advice you're going to get based on who you ask. Ask someone who went to business school to get their MBA if you should get your MBA or not, and guess what they'll say. Conversely, ask someone who never went back to get their MBA whether or not you should pursue an MBA, and guess what they'll say.

There's no one way to succeed, and there is very rarely one way of doing things. No one's advice will be perfect for **you**.

Luckily for you, this doesn't mean that you can't get help or you can't solicit opinions and perspectives from other people, but the point is that in the beginning you should be willing to learn on your own, fail on your own, and succeed on your own. You'll learn a lot more that way, and you'll learn it a lot faster.

The Most Important Factor When Starting

Above all else, when starting anything – especially your business – you need to understand what the most important factor is when it comes to starting anything.

YOU! You are the single most important factor when it comes to starting a business. At the end of the day, you need to stop looking out the window for success and start looking in the mirror. You are the only person who can bring you success, and you are the only person who can decide when you fail. After all, the only way to fail is to quit.

The last story I'll leave you with in this chapter is that of Lisa Nichols. At the age of 27, Lisa was the mother of a child whose father was in prison, in the rough environments of inner city Los Angeles.

With no strong academic background (she never got above a C in school) to lift herself to new heights and opportunities, Lisa reached rock bottom when she one day couldn't afford to buy diapers for her son.

Rather than looking out her window for success, Lisa looked in the mirror, and found a job.

"I felt rock bottom, and I realized, 'I have to do something,'" Nichols told the *Today Show* in an interview in 2014. "I have to be my own rescue. No one's going to rescue me."

With the income from her job, Lisa saved up for a dream opportunity. At the time Lisa didn't have an idea what the dream would be, but she knew that saving up would leave her well-positioned in the future.

In the end, her savings allowed her to start

"Motivating the Teen Spirit," which gave her a platform to travel to conferences around the country and speak to youth about making positive choices in life.

"Motivating the Teen Spirit" turned into "Motivating the Masses," which is a collection of training resources that Lisa has put together. "Motivating the Masses" has been so successful that it was featured in the best-selling book *The Secret*, and has turned Lisa into one of the most sought-after motivational speakers in the world. On top of that, Lisa has published six best-selling books of her own, and she has reached and served nearly 30 million people. How's that for impact!?

Lisa's story reiterates the importance of being naïve and starting before you're ready (she started saving when she didn't even know what she was saving for), as well as looking in the mirror for change.

2

The Ultimate Decider of Success: Mindset

When starting a business, it's easy to think about the tangible things: your product/service, your customers, and your processes. More important than all of these things, though, is an intangible variable: your mindset.

There are so many books, videos, trainings, seminars, and courses out there about mindset, and 99% of entrepreneurs skip this crucial ingredient. I personally have been guilty of this, because at the beginning of starting a business you have what seems like much bigger things to worry about.

Indeed, it's possible to experience some level of success without the proper mindset, but when a business plateaus it all comes down to mindset... whether that's a revenue plateau, a product improvement plateau, or a plateau in terms of work hours.

This book is certainly not meant to be some fluffy book about how your positive thoughts can manifest money (because, quite frankly, without action they can't), but no book about becoming an entrepreneur would be complete without at least touching on some of the struggles that every entrepreneur is certain to encounter.

There will be "Dips"

Seth Godin, one of the most innovative thinkers in the world of entrepreneurship, has an entire book dedicated to what he calls "the dip." Seth defines a dip as a moment in any journey or project where the challenges are high and the likelihood of quitting is increased.

In his book, aptly named *The Dip: A Little Book that Teaches You When to Quit*, Seth uses tennis as an example to illustrate what the dip is. Seth argues that the difference between average tennis players and international superstars like Roger Federer isn't natural talent — it's the "ability to push through the moments where it's just easier to quit."

To Seth's point, at one point in time you and I were both as good at tennis as Roger Federer. Suppose we went to take tennis lessons; at the beginning we'd see massive improvements on a daily basis. We'd essentially be going from zero to one; having had no experience or strategy when it comes to serving the ball, we'd make marked improvements in a short period of time.

After getting a solid foundation through lessons, however, we'd hit a plateau, where further improvements require more work, more energy, and aren't immediately apparent. Inevitably, when we go months without visible improvements, frustration begins to mount, and it becomes easier to quit than to continue showing up every single day.

Guys like Roger Federer plowed through the dip for years, and that's why they're the best in the world at what they do. The rest of us quit when we hit the dip, so we weren't even in the game long enough to compete with the best.

Luckily for you and I, the dip creates scarcity, which allows us to succeed in the marketplace. The dips cause people to quit. It's for this reason that most businesses fail; rather than trudging through the dips, they quit when it stops being fun.

To further illustrate the dip in action, I want to tell you a real-life story about a man who had only $106 in the bank, a pregnant wife, and a starving dog that he couldn't afford to feed. On top of his woes, he lived in an apartment that he couldn't afford to pay rent on.

In the face of financial ruin, this guy decided to spend the next three and a half days writing a script for a movie starring himself. That was the fun and easy part... surely there were parts where he had writer's block, but there was no rejection involved in just sitting down and writing a movie script. This is something that you can do right now if you wanted to.

From there, though, the challenge of becoming a movie star became more difficult. After writing the script, this guy had to *sell* the script, and sell *himself* as the star of the film.

When attempting to sell the script, time and time again studios showed interest, but were adamant that the man himself could not be the star of the film. Unfortunately for the writer, he had a speech impediment and a physical appearance that was less than ideal for a starring role on the big screens thanks to complications at birth.

The writer faced many dips in his journey to getting a studio to purchase the rights to the movie, including a starring role, and very easily could have quit by simply selling the script without the promise of the starring role.

Instead, he sold it at a tiny fraction of his initial offers in order to secure the starring role. Having rejected offers upwards of $250,000 for his script, in the end the financially-strapped writer held out for less than $50,000 so that he could star in the movie himself.

Had he quit in his pursuit to be a movie star and accepted the initial offer (which would have been easier), the world may never have been blessed with knowing the talents and drive of this guy.

His name was Sylvester Stallone, and the movie that he wrote was called *Rocky*.

The Imposter Syndrome

Without a doubt, every single entrepreneur struggles with the imposter syndrome. This happens at all stages of entrepreneurship, from the beginning and all throughout the journey.

At its most basic level, the "imposter syndrome" is when you feel like you're not qualified enough to be doing what you're doing, causing you to feel like an imposter. For example, when I was 19 years old and went to a professional match on a press pass for the first time ever (it was AC Milan vs. Inter Milan, two of the biggest clubs in Italian soccer), I had the strong feeling that I didn't deserve to be there.

"Who am I to be covering this match and talking to these players?" I asked myself while standing on the sidelines. I kept reminding myself that I had no formal training or education in journalism, and I had never even covered a sporting event live before. Yet here I was standing on the field with some of the biggest names in the world of soccer. If anyone there felt like an imposter, it was me.

I wasted most of the day not talking to anyone, and made myself so nervous that the first question I asked to Clarence Seedorf, one of the most decorated players in European soccer history, was immediately squashed and ridiculed by the player. "That's a terrible question," he replied after I asked him if the motivation of the World Cup would give him a greater incentive to work even harder this season.

It may or may not have been a great question (in the end, he didn't make Holland's World Cup squad, so maybe it was!), but Seedorf's sharp reply confirmed the fact that I was indeed "just a blogger." I wanted to roll up and hide in a corner deep within the tunnels of Gillette Stadium.

I could have let that define me and define the ceiling of Premiership Talk (my soccer website), but instead I was fortunate enough to be in a great mindset to push on. Sometimes when it comes to mindset, all you need is a little win to get you over the hump.

In entrepreneurship it's popular to give advice like "move towards your fear to overcome it," but I've always liked to use the approach of moving towards something safe when you need to celebrate a win.

After Clarence Seedorf shut me down, I opted for a safer approach to help me get over my recent rejection, so decided to approach then-AC Milan defender Oguchi Onyewu, the only American on either roster. Surely it would be easier to interview a fellow American rather than players who only speak English as their second, third, or fourth language!

Indeed, it was much easier. Oguchi was patient, insightful, and generous, and his answers gave me some great stories to run with. Small wins can certainly help shift your mindset, so it's important to look for them when times are tough.

Back onto the topic of the imposter syndrome, though. It's easy to feel like an imposter when you put yourself out there. I've spoken at countless seminars and conferences, but every once in a while I still think to myself, "who am I to be telling these people how to build a successful business? I'm still not where I want to be, and there are entrepreneurs far more successful than I am. Why should they listen to me?"

Honestly, there's no good answer to the imposter syndrome, other than acknowledging that it exists so that you can spot it and move past it. When you start your business, you clearly have the confidence to push forward, but as time goes on that confidence wanes, causing you to question if you are "good enough" or "smart enough" or "successful enough" to do whatever it is that you're doing. And indeed you are. If you're taking action then you're already ahead of 99% of the population, so you're not an imposter.

One of my favorite students that I've worked with was known as the "voice of soccer in America." This guy was one of the pioneers in soccer coverage in the United States during the 2000s, and almost every soccer fan could recognize his voice and his face after seeing him so much on television.

After his days on television were over, he became my student as he wanted to start building an online empire of soccer coaching tutorials and resources. In addition to being an immediately recognizable television personality, this particular student is a US Soccer A-Licensed coach (the highest coaching license you can hold in the USA), and an assistant coach for one of the best Olympic Development Programs in the country. In short, he had all the credentials.

When it came time to build his online empire, the imposter syndrome struck him hard at almost every step of the process. He made the giant mistake of Googling his "competition" to see what they did, and once he saw their course outlines he immediately became self-conscious of his own ability to deliver similar content.

To get him over this hump, I constantly asked him questions such as "do you really believe this guy is better than you?" "No" was the answer every time.

"So if he can do it, then give me one good reason why you can't." That's a harder one to answer.

But, sure enough, in a few days when this particular student hit another dip – maybe he was struggling to sit down and find a groove, or maybe life was just getting in the way and throwing him off – the imposter syndrome would strike again.

"But Brian, why would anyone buy these coaching

resources from *me*? Who am *I* to be putting all of this together?"

I loved this question, because it had an easy answer. "Who is [competitor's name]? Why should anyone listen to him? Because he puts his work out there, and he knows more than they do. You shouldn't expect the best coaches in the world to benefit from your stuff, because you're right, maybe they wouldn't and shouldn't listen to you. But you're ahead of 99% of the population, so *that's* who should listen to you."

It worked every time.

One of my favorite movies of all time is *Catch Me if You Can*, starring Leonardo DiCaprio. DiCaprio plays the role of Frank Abagnale, who is widely regarded as the greatest con man of all time. A "con man" is nothing more than an imposter, so looking at Abagnale's story is certain to give insight into how to get over the imposter syndrome. After all, this is a guy who flew over a million miles for free after pretending to be an airline pilot. Rather than believing he wasn't "good enough" to be a pilot, he had to mentally position himself and lie to *himself* so that he could convince *others* that he was a pilot.

One of Frank's most widely discussed (and debated) cons was when he allegedly impersonated a professor and taught a class at the prestigious BYU (Brigham Young University) in Utah. According to Abagnale, whose cons were so grand that he found himself on the FBI's most wanted list, he convinced the university that he was a sociology professor and ended up teaching a class for one semester.

"I was hired within the hour to teach two six-week semesters during the summer at a salary of $1,600 per semester," Abagnale claimed. "I was assigned to teach a ninety-minute freshman course in the morning, three days a week...

"There were 78 students in my freshman class and 63 students in my sophomore course... At least fifty of my students sought me out to tell me how much they had enjoyed my classes."

When asked how he could successfully pose as a sociology professor, having no formal education in the field, Frank had a simple explanation.

"It wasn't difficult, I read one chapter ahead of my students. They never knew the difference," Abagnale states.

Frank's point of only needing to read one chapter ahead makes perfect sense, and is the perfect antidote to the imposter syndrome. When faced with the imposter syndrome – or, in simple terms, any time you ask "who am I to do this" or "who am I to get paid to do this?" – just remember that you're at least one chapter ahead of whoever you're working with or whoever is paying you.

One of my proudest accomplishments as a champion of newpreneurs came in 2014 when I successfully helped a student launch his own photography and videography business. Sensing a yearning to be creative for the first time in his life, I worked one on one with this student to find his passion. Having just picked up photography as a hobby, I was eager to talk to anyone and everyone about my new camera (like him, I was yearning for a creative outlet, and was having a blast with my first DSLR camera).

While he had no formal photography training, he clearly had an eye for a shot with his basic smartphone camera, so I was thrilled to show him what I learned about using a DSLR for photography. By no means was I an outstanding photographer (nor am I today!), but I had been the proud owner of a Nikon camera for three months at that point. So, I taught him all about what I had already learned... aperture, ISO, shutter speeds, camera equipment, different techniques, you name it, and I was happy to share my limited knowledge!

Keep in mind, I have zero formal experience with photography, and I'm sure to a trained eye my pictures are riddled with errors. *But,* when it came to showing this student how to use a DSLR camera, I was a few chapters ahead, and that's all I needed to be able to teach him.

He learned a lot in a short amount of time, and soon blew past my own limited knowledge of cameras. A few months later he landed his first $3,000 photography client, and his business was officially born.

Had I hesitated in teaching him because I "wasn't qualified" – which, by all means, I wasn't – then his business might not exist today. There's immense power in learning from someone who is just one chapter ahead.

While the point might already be made, I want to give one final perspective on being "one chapter ahead." Had this student learned from the best photographer in the world, he might not have enjoyed such quick results. The best photographer in the world might focus on more technical, artistic elements of creating a good shot, whereas this student needed the bare-bone basics before progressing on to the more advanced stuff. For the best photographer in the world, this stuff might be second nature, so he may not have covered it as well as I had. My training was essential textbook training, as I literally learned just weeks before passing my limited education on.

Similarly, world famous business development coach Tony Robbins could likely teach me a thing or two about business. But chances are I could learn even more – and get even better results – by working with someone who is just one or two steps ahead of me in my quest to grow a seven-figure business. Why? Because someone who is closer to where I am would better understand my current challenges and guide me through those, whereas someone like Tony

Robbins might forget what it's like to be in the stage that I'm at in my business.

The moral of this story is that you'll undoubtedly be faced with the imposter syndrome many times throughout your journey as an entrepreneur. The challenge is to identify it, acknowledge it, and ask yourself if you're at least "one chapter ahead." If so, then the people who are one chapter behind you would be thrilled to gain your knowledge. That's where your value in the marketplace is.

The Art of the Hustle

This chapter is all about mindset, so when thinking about the most important aspect of what an entrepreneur's mental state needs to be, only one word comes to mind: **hustle.**

Being an entrepreneur means being a hustler. If you're not ready to hustle day in and day out, then I promise you won't be successful. I know that the "four hour work week" is a popular aim, but guys like Tim Ferriss (author of the bestselling book *The Four Hour Work Week*) had to hustle for many years to make that possible. Tim had to work day in and day out, which sometimes means missing out on concerts with friends, missing major sporting events, missing parties, and missing out on entire series of your favorite television show.

The number one way to identify if someone is a hustler or not is to see if they use the "I don't have time" excuse. I understand how difficult it is to find time to start a business, especially if you're working a full-time job. I started Premiership Talk when I was entering my sophomore year of college, so I had nothing but time on my hands.

But once I started it, I pushed everything to the side and hustled around the clock to make it a success. I went many months with practically zero readers other than my parents, my girlfriend, my roommate, and a few of my friends. I didn't care; I persisted.

I spent countless nights up all night in the school library writing blog posts, redoing my website, sending emails to other bloggers, and researching techniques on how to grow my blog. I didn't have time to watch TV, I didn't play as many video games as I would have liked, and I can count the number of college parties that I attended on one hand.

This is definitely not meant to be a story about how much I missed in college. In fact, I wouldn't switch a single thing about my college experience. I may have actually missed *more* things in order to hustle even *harder*. Because in the end, the experiences that I *did* have while I was "missing" these things are far more rewarding. While I was "missing" college parties, I was flying to England to pick up a prestigious award from the English Football Association. While I was "missing" certain school events that "everyone was going to," I was securing press credentials to see the world's top soccer players compete in places like Miami, Washington DC, and New York.

And don't get me started on sleep. I *loooooove* a good night's rest. Sleeping is glorious. Especially in the colder months, sprawling out on a comfortable bed covered in blankets is the best experience in the world. But guess what… I missed out on sleep. I pulled more all-nighters than I can count, constantly writing new content, making new connections, and expanding Prem Talk's content distribution channels. Ah yes, think about all of those hours of sleep that I "missed out on."

So the question is… did I want to succeed as badly as I wanted to sleep? Did I want to succeed as badly as I wanted to go to a few more college parties? Did I want to succeed as badly as I wanted to play video games? Yes – I wanted to succeed more than anything, so I put the work in. And in hindsight, so many of my classmates envy the number of countries I've been to, the people I've met, the revenue I've generated, and the lifestyle that I've built for myself. They envy it, but they didn't want it as badly as they wanted to party, watch TV, and play video games. Everyone wants the results, but no one wants to do the work.

Thanks to student loans and the pressures of society's expectations, I felt like I needed to get a "real job" upon graduation in 2011. I clearly was never cut out for corporate America and a one-hour commute each way, but I tried to play Mr. Corporate America for a while, at the expense of growing Prem Talk further. (Being a "blogger" wasn't as acceptable at the time, and there were giant concerns about the long-term stability of online advertising revenue, especially in the face of more widespread ad-blockers)

A few months into my first job, I knew corporate America wasn't for me, so I decided to jump back into the world of entrepreneurship. I decided to accept a much higher-paying job with the vision of collecting as much money as possible while building my business on the side.

It was during this time – working a 9 to 5 – that I truly learned the art of the hustle. "Hustling" in college is one thing, but hustling as an adult is a totally different experience. Rather than having to go to class for a few hours a day, I had the real responsibility of student loans, a commute, bills, and dedicating at least 40 hours a week to performing well at a job.

So many wantrepreneurs find themselves stuck in a 9 to 5, and I totally understand that. I've been there. And so many times I hear the excuse "I don't have enough time because of my job."

That's BS. That's nothing more than an excuse.

Suppose you have a one-hour commute each way

(which is generous, because the national average is lower than that, but I'll be nice and round up), that means that your job takes up the hours of 8am to 6pm (10 hours total). Let's suppose that dinner takes another hour – we're now at 7pm. Let's suppose it takes you **two hours** to wind down – we're now at 9pm. Keep in mind, I've been *very* generous with these numbers – two hours of "winding down" time means two hours to do whatever it is that you want to do: exercise, watch TV, spend time with your significant other, walk the dog, run errands, etc.

What do you do with the rest of your night? What do you do between 9pm and midnight? That's where you can hustle. Whenever I hear someone say they don't have enough time, this picture clearly illustrates that even with these responsibilities, it's possible to find just three hours of time per night to work on your business. Three hours per night adds up to 15 hours per week spent growing your business, plus whatever time you can spend on weekends.

"But Brian, what about sleep?" Look – in the above example, you can easily still get six or seven hours of sleep. And I'm fully aware that that's below the eight hours of sleep that we all want, but the question is easy – do you want to succeed as badly as you want to sleep? Are you willing to sacrifice a little sleep to setup the rest of your life to be one that you've always dreamed of?

There's a famous quote that says "If you don't make the time to work on creating the life you want, you're eventually going to be forced to spend a LOT of time dealing with a life you don't want."

Quite simply, if you have time to watch TV, play video games, sleep eight hours a night, read pointless articles on the internet, or watch silly videos on YouTube, then you have enough time to **hustle**. People who "don't have enough time" just don't want to succeed as badly as they want to do those other pointless things.

My good friend Greg Faxon, who quit his job when he was just 22 years old and now runs a successful coaching business, made a great point when he was a speaker at the 2015 IM Summit, an event which I launched and hosted. Greg argues that when people say they don't have the time, it has nothing to do with time, only motivation. Greg asks wantrepreneurs, "if I offered you a million dollars to find the time, would you be able to?" Realistically, if a million dollars was on the line, I'm willing to bet that you could find the time, which proves that indeed, this isn't a question of time, but a question of motivation.

"People who are unable to motivate themselves must be content with mediocrity, no matter how impressive their other talents."

It's in Your Hands

The coolest part about being an entrepreneur is that you control your own destiny. The scariest part about being an entrepreneur is that you control your own destiny.

Ultimately as an entrepreneur, it's **you** who decides how successful you'll be, if you'll fail, how hard you work, who you work with, what tasks you do, and where you go. There is no one there to tell you what you need to do, there's no one there to push you to work harder, and there's no one there to hold your hand.

The biggest mistake that I see newpreneurs make is they attach their wagon to someone else's star and hope that they get taken along for a ride. Newpreneurs often find mentors in their local communities or online that are willing to show them the next steps, but that often creates a false sense of ownership and shared responsibility. As someone who has mentored and helped many newpreneurs in the past, I've been extremely cautious and aware of when these new entrepreneurs start counting on someone other than themselves to make things happen.

I used to help out newpreneurs all the time, until I realized that they're better off being helped from afar. One entrepreneur who I worked with came to me desperate and hungry for his own entrepreneurial adventure. He wanted to start an online community of video gamers, and was asking me for advice on how to secure startup funding to get the website made. I was thrilled to see his enthusiasm and passion for the project as he wrote up his multiple revenue streams, traffic sources, and expansion plans for the website, so as a former web designer I figured I'd give him a break and create the website for him for free. I can't resist helping newpreneurs out.

I spent a few days creating the website and membership platform for him, and he was absolutely thrilled that he now had a functioning site that he could use at the beginning to at least build up his userbase and establish his first revenue stream.

When I checked back in with him a month later to see how he was attracting users, he indicated that he needed some help with Facebook Ads to drive traffic to his website. Again, I was more than happy to help out (despite the fact that no progress was made over the past month), and walked him through the process step by step. Days later, he reached out to see if I could help him analyze the Facebook Ads campaign. Happy to do so, I showed him that the traffic was indeed converting, but suggested that he start producing content and coming up with ideas to **retain** those users.

In the end, he only took action when I probed him and asked how things were going, at which point I questioned who was really growing this business. That encounter, among others, taught me two things:

1) Newpreneurs are better off on their own, perhaps

asking for advice along the way, but handling 100% of the execution themselves as they'll be better off in the long run. And,

2) Most newpreneurs are lacking the key ingredients of being a **self-starter** and **committing to do something every single day** to build their business

One of the most important parts of getting your mindset right at the beginning is making that huge commitment of doing something every single day.

Every. Single. Day.

"The first step towards getting somewhere is to decide that you are not going to stay where you are."

While there are a lot of nuggets of knowledge and insights in the above few paragraphs, the important thing to understand is that ultimately **you** are responsible for everything – not just in your business, but in your life. The sooner you accept that fact, the sooner you can succeed.

"If you're searching for that one person that will change your life, take a look in the mirror."

This means that you're responsible for the good things that happen to you, as well as the bad things that happen to you. Make the decision today to do work every single day that moves you forward in your pursuit of success and the life that you want.

Do you find yourself waiting for someone else to get back to you in order to move forward? Do you find yourself waiting for someone else to show you how to do something in order to move forward?

Stop waiting, and take responsibility for yourself. You shouldn't be waiting for anyone else to grow **your** business. Google whatever it is that you need to learn – I guarantee there's a free resource. Do you need to create a website?

Google it. Do you need to create a logo? Google it.

There's a time and a place to outsource things and to pay other people to do things for you, but at the beginning it helps to bootstrap, which means to put on your boots and head into the field yourself. "Bootstrapping" is becoming more and more popular within the startup scene, because it's the most cost-effective and efficient way to get a business off the ground. On top of that, you'll gain skills and experience that will pay off time and time again in the future in ways that you can't even imagine.

You don't need startup money, and you don't need anyone else. Yet.

Be Ready to Test Your Limits

In 1954 something impossible happened. For decades – maybe centuries! – people believed that running a mile in less than four minutes was impossible. On May 6th, 1954, Roger Bannister did what no human had ever done before... he ran a mile in 3 minutes and 59.4 seconds.

Leading up to Roger Bannister's "impossible" feat, many people were certain that such a fast mile was beyond the capabilities of the human body. The name that most people don't know in this story, however, is John Landy, an Australian runner who broke Bannister's record only a month later, running the mile in just 3 minutes and 57.9 seconds.

What John – and the world – needed was just for someone to show them what was possible, and then it was widely accepted as something attainable. Indeed, after these two men showed the world that running a sub-four minute mile was attainable, it became more and more common, to the point where today there are **high-schoolers** that can run a mile in less than four minutes!

These sort of artificial barriers are seen everywhere in the world, not just in sports. Growing up, I was always fascinated by those invisible electric dog fences. As a kid who was always slightly afraid of dogs, I rejoiced when these invisible fences started becoming popular, as they saved me from having to worry about dogs chasing me down the street as I rode my bicycle around town.

In case you're not familiar with these, many suburban homeowners started installing invisible electric fences around the perimeters of their property to keep their dogs from running away. The dogs had a special device attached to their collars, so if they tried to cross the invisible electric fence they'd get shocked and retreat.

Obviously, because the fences are invisible, every dog would experience such a shock at least once in their life. After all, without being able to see the fence, they only learned of its existence by experiencing the shock. (For the less intelligent dogs, it took more than one shock for them to learn about the new invisible barriers!)

One of my friend's families had the invisible fence installed on their property, and it didn't take long for their dog to learn its boundaries. Years later, I remember hearing my friend's parents talk about how the fence no longer "worked." The electric field had stopped working long before (after a few winters and construction in the neighborhood), but the fence still "worked" in the sense that their dog **never** ran off the property.

Despite the fact that the electric field had stopped working, the barrier still existed within the dog's mind after one or two bad experiences of getting shocked.

As entrepreneurs (and maybe just as people!), we all have these artificial barriers in our lives. Maybe someone once told you that they knew of a business similar to yours that went bankrupt, so you've built the artificial barrier in your own mind to convince yourself that your idea can't work. Or maybe you put yourself out on a limb before and it didn't pay off, so you're afraid to take risks now. Whatever your situation may be, in order to get in the right mindset for success, it's important to assess what your artificial barriers are that could potentially serve as roadblocks.

As Roger Bannister and John Landy proved, everything is impossible... until it's possible.

What limiting beliefs do you have? An easy way to discover your own artificial barriers is to ask yourself, "why can't I accomplish [insert your measurement of success here]?"

Maybe your answer is "because people can't make money with [insert your passion here]." Or maybe your answer is "I don't have enough money to make that happen," or "I don't have the connections to make that happen."

You know what? None of that matters. I can absolutely guarantee you that there's someone who came from a worse-off situation than you that made it, because they didn't let their beliefs limit what was possible for them.

Test your beliefs... I'm willing to bet that you've built **artificial** barriers in your own mind.

And if you did have a truly bad experience with something in the past and you believe that that is still an obstacle for you today, then remember that just because a door was locked yesterday doesn't mean it's locked today. Re-test your beliefs and see if they still hold true. And even if they do, there's always a way around every obstacle, so success **is** possible, but only if you commit and **believe** that it's possible.

"Whether you think you can or you can't, you're right."

Do the Stuff that Hurts

Muhammad Ali is widely regarded as the greatest heavyweight boxer of all time. On his way to becoming a world champion, Ali said many brilliant things about winning and about determination, such as "the fight is won or lost far away from witnesses – behind the lines, in the gym, and out there on the road, long before I dance under those lights."

But despite all of his great quotes, the one that stands out for me was in an interview when he was asked how many sit-ups he does per day. Muhammed Ali replied: "I don't count my sit-ups. I only start counting when it starts hurting. That is when I start counting, because then it really counts. That's what makes you a champion."

Every entrepreneur – no matter what stage they're at – can find inspiration in that quote.

Along the same lines as that quote, if you go to the gym everyday and only do 10 reps and don't feel any of the pain, then chances are you're not making any gains.

Entrepreneurs, perhaps more than any other group of professionals, need to do the things that hurt. Newpreneurs fall into the trap of expecting immediate results, and their early excitement quickly fades if they don't experience early success.

I've lost track of the number of times I've come across wantrepreneurs who said "Oh, I tried starting my own business, but it never really took off." Naturally, I can't help but ask how long they tried, and it always pains me when they say they "tried" for less than a year.

During your first year or so, entrepreneurship especially hurts. You face what is perhaps the most difficult challenge of all: getting your business to the point where it has income that can sustain your lifestyle. Different challenges (also known as "opportunities") present themselves further down the road in entrepreneurship, but those challenges are much easier to face when you already have income coming in and know that you can survive another day financially.

I'm not suggesting that *every* entrepreneur will have a painful first year in existence. Nor does it have to be a year of struggle – it could be much shorter, or it could be much longer. But what I'm informing you of now, while you're still transitioning to becoming an entrepreneur, is that the beginning takes a lot of work, and at times it will hurt.

You're guaranteed to deal with a lot of challenges. **But nothing you do matters** unless you can feel it hurting. So you approached one potential client and they said no to working with you? Don't you dare chalk that up as a failure, and don't you dare let that impact your future as an entrepreneur. That doesn't even hurt yet… that's one no. (And if one no hurts you, then maybe entrepreneurship isn't for you – there will be more no's to come!)

Most new entrepreneurs quit right when they're one hurdle away from success… and the sad part is that they never realize it. I can guarantee that there was a soccer website out there better than mine at the same time that I started Prem Talk, but I persisted, even when it hurt and I was spending (and it felt like *wasting*) well over 40 hours a week working on a website that no one visited. But, somewhere, that website that was better than mine decided to quit due to a lack of readership, as they weren't prepared to endure the pain and sacrifice – and **rewards** – that entrepreneurship poses.

Are you ready to commit to putting the work in every single day? And remember that none of it counts up-front until you push through the pain?

Decide that you want to succeed as an entrepreneur, and commit to doing what it takes to get there.

When you're deciding what to do next to grow your business and you're looking at your task list, categorize each activity into one of two buckets: **towards fear**, or **towards** comfort.

Activities that are moving **towards comfort** are the easy things that don't involve putting yourself out there. Some of these activities include creating or choosing a new logo for your business, updating your website, setting up your email signature, posting on Facebook, creating a Facebook business page, playing around on Instagram, and creating business cards. These activities *might* be necessary for your business (although even that's debatable), but none of them will significantly move your business forward.

Activities that involve **moving towards fear,** however, are the things that can really push you forward. These are activities where you're uncomfortable, and where you risk the threat of rejection and/or failure. Such activities are sales conversations, reaching out to potential partners who are much bigger and more established than you, speaking at conferences or seminars, and arranging your own events. The list is much longer based on what your specific business is, but the common thread among all of these activities is that they're less comfortable and less safe compared to the comfort tasks that I listed above.

These activities, despite being painful, are the ones that can produce the most results in your life and in your business. These are the activities that truly move your business forward and bring in revenues.

Your mindset needs to be one where you embrace fear, acknowledge it, and then tackle it.

What Do You Want?

We'll close this mindset chapter out by talking about a very important decision that you need to make, which will frame your entire mindset as an entrepreneur.

Before you can enjoy any level of success, you need to decide **what exactly do you want?**

The human brain is an interesting machine. I'm no psychology major, but over the years of running my own businesses I've chosen to spend some time learning about how the brain works so I can hack it and use it to my advantage.

Here's a fun exercise to do to see how fascinating the brain is. Look around the room that you're sitting in right now, and for 60 seconds try to memorize every single thing in the room that is black. Seriously – go ahead and do it. Look the room over so intensely that you memorize everything that is black.

I'll give you some time to actually do this exercise…

Come on…

Okay, don't read ahead until you've done this exercise…

Alright, so hopefully you've spent 60 seconds looking around the room. Now that you're reading this book again, without looking away from the book, **tell me everything you saw that is blue.**

If you're like most people, your brain just got frazzled in that moment, because you were so tuned in to the black objects in the room that you completely looked over all of the blue objects, despite the fact that you very intently studied everything in the room.

This, in my opinion, is the most interesting feature of the brain. The reason why that exercise was so difficult is because our brains have a feature called the reticular activating system (**RAS**). The RAS is the system in your brain that triggers your attention when something is of interest to you. In the example above, your RAS was turned on to black objects because I told you to pay attention to them, so those stood out above all the other things that were right there in front of your eyes.

Have you ever gotten a new car, and then all of a sudden seen that car everywhere on the road? Or maybe you were *thinking* about buying a new car, and from that point forward that's all you noticed on the road? You can turn your RAS on to anything that you can imagine, and your brain will start noticing that more than anything else, even when other things are in plain sight.

What this has to do with you and I as entrepreneurs is that we need absolute clarity on what it is that we want, otherwise the perfect opportunity could be hiding in plain sight. When I was running NewGen Consultants, a marketing agency that I founded in 2012, at the beginning we hadn't taken the time to get clarity on what we wanted. This meant we took on any and all projects that came our way, even if those projects moved us farther away from what we eventually wanted (freedom, traveling, and our dream lifestyle).

Sooner or later, by saying "yes" to projects that pulled us away from what we really wanted, we started to hate our business. I can very clearly recall an emotional conversation that I had with my business partner one beautiful fall day, when we both realized that we were pushing forward without any sort of clarity.

After deciding on what we wanted, that clarity allowed our reticular activating systems to immediately pinpoint the opportunities and directions that most closely aligned with our desired situations and lifestyles. From there, rather than taking on tedious website development projects that weren't rewarding for us and that involved tedious aspects of back and forth with clients, we decided to focus our energies on traveling throughout the northeast United States to lead seminars and workshops, and from those we identified our dream clients.

Part of your mindset in your early days as an

entrepreneur **must be** focused around getting clarity on what exactly you want. This advice should be heeded when it comes to what's good for your business as well. By achieving clarity on what your long-term business objectives are, your brain's RAS will reveal those opportunities to you, without you even looking for them specifically.

Anything is Possible

In this chapter we've spent a lot of time talking about the mindset of an entrepreneur, but at the end of the day there's one thing that you really need to understand: **anything is possible**.

To illustrate this, I want to take you back to 1990. A young comic in Los Angeles was becoming increasingly frustrated with his floundering comedic career, especially after a life where his family was so poor that at one point they lived in a Volkswagen van on a relative's lawn. On this particular night in 1990, this comic drove to the top of a hill in his old, falling apart Toyota, and decided to write a check to himself for $10 million. In the memo field, he wrote "For acting services rendered," despite the fact that there was no path to such money – or such a career – in sight.

The check was dated for Thanksgiving Day, 1995, and was put into his wallet.

Fast forward five years later, and that comic had gone from an impoverished starving comic to one of the most successful comedy actors in Hollywood, starring in films such as *Ace Ventura*, *The Mask*, and *Liar, Liar*.

If you couldn't tell by now, that starving comic was Jim Carrey, and his story shows how it's possible to go from being homeless to a world-renowned success story in just a matter of years when you **make the conscious decision** to not accept the situation that was handed to you.

Today, as you take the necessary steps to finally

launch, build, and grow the business that you've always dreamed of, **decide** that you're going to change your fortunes and change your life story. Write yourself **permission to succeed**.

3

Your Scarcest Resource: Focus

In the first two chapters, we laid a lot of the groundwork about the mental state required to build a successful business. In this chapter, I'm going to reveal the single most important factor of your success (other than simply **taking action**).

Most people – new entrepreneurs and established entrepreneurs alike – find this key ingredient to be a constant challenge, and it's for this reason that most entrepreneurs fail before they ever succeed.

This key ingredient is **FOCUS**.

One of the most inspiring entrepreneurs that I've had the pleasure of spending time with is John Lee Dumas. John's first business was a business podcast called *Entrepreneur on Fire*. Entrepreneur on Fire is a seven-day-a-week podcast where John interviews successful entrepreneurs from all different industries, and was named the iTunes Podcast of the Year in 2013.

The cool thing about John is that he publishes monthly income reports to show the community how much revenue he's making, what his expenses are, how he plans to grow his revenues in the future, and what he spends his money on. To give you an idea of his success, in October 2015 (just three years after the launch of his podcast), John revealed that he grossed over $540,000 in revenue that month alone. With almost $100,000 in expenses, though, his **net profits** for that one month were $453,586. How's that for growing a business quickly!?

In the summer of 2014 I went to a summer camp in upstate New York with John, and played soccer with him for a couple of hours. During this time, I asked him for his secret to success.

He didn't even hesitate for a second.

"Focus," was his immediate response.

John is quite open on his podcast about the importance of focus. In fact, he frequently says that FOCUS is an acronym standing for **Follow One Course Until Success**. I particularly like how he says "until," because so many entrepreneurs follow certain strategies or tactics, but then quit before they ever have the chance to succeed with it.

Since the day he launched his podcast, John has been laser-focused on making his podcast succeed. And, he's persisted day in and day out **until** it has succeeded. Rather than chasing new shiny objects and new revenue streams that become flashes in the pan, John decided that he was going to run a successful podcast, and that focus never wavered, making Entrepreneur on Fire one of the most well-known and most listened to podcasts in the world.

John's laser-sharp focus impacts every area of his business. When he first toyed with the idea of a seven-day-a-week podcast, many people in the industry told him it wouldn't be possible and that he'd get burned out creating that many episodes. Now, over 1,100 episodes in, John has never missed a day, regardless of how crazy his schedule gets or how much he travels.

A key part of that has been John's method of batch processing. John dedicates one day a week to doing upwards of ten podcast interviews, so he is not only all set for the week, but he also builds up an extensive catalog of future episodes. By doing this, John gets an entire week of episodes done in just one day, so the rest of the week he can focus on other business-building activities, such as responding to emails, dealing with advertisers, and building out his long-term business strategy.

The most impressive thing that I've seen John do in his business is **focus** on his customer avatar.

If you're not familiar with the idea of a customer avatar then you need to be, as this is the **single most important thing to decide on in your business**. No book about going from wantrepreneur to entrepreneur would be complete without establishing the importance of building out a **customer avatar**.

A customer avatar is the **one person** who you are aiming to serve with your business. It's not a target market – it's one person, with one age, one name, and one set of behaviors, demographics, interests, and background.

To give you a real life example, John's customer avatar is named Jimmy. Jimmy has a 35 minute commute to work, and hates listening to commercials on the radio. In addition to those two traits, John has a detailed document that is pages long that details who Jimmy is. By doing this, John knows **exactly** what direction to take his business in, and can focus on best serving his customer avatar.

You might be wondering how to come up with your own customer avatar. The question you need to answer is: **Who do I want to serve? Who will best resonate with my business, my products, my services, and my messaging/voice?** The key thing to remember is that your customer avatar is one person, and in many cases it can be a previous version of yourself. It can also be a customer or client of yours, or even someone that you make up.

Most people hesitate to build out a customer avatar and build their entire business around one person because they don't want to narrow their potential customer base. What you need to remember is that by doing this, you are **not** narrowing your potential audience. Instead, you're narrowing your focus so you can best serve the market.

Indeed, people who aren't just like Jimmy also listen to Entrepreneur on Fire, and in my own business, I have thousands of students who are different from who my customer avatar is. **But** – my customer avatar still drives my focus and drives my decisions on how I grow my business.

What Your Only Focus Is

As an entrepreneur, there's no one to tell you what to do. There's no one to give you assignments, lay out projects for you, or stay on top of you to ensure you're moving in the right direction.

That's the biggest plus of being an entrepreneur, but also one of the biggest challenges.

The facts are simple, though. As an entrepreneur, you really should only have three main focuses: solving a problem, finding leads, and turning those leads into customers. Of course, within each of these areas is a series of responsibilities, but at its most basic level you need to be focusing on each of these things.

"Solving a problem" is the core of your business. Pick any company, and they solve a problem. Coca-Cola solves the problem of people wanting a satisfying and delicious soft-drink, Amazon solves the problem of consumers wanting a convenient, affordable retailer for everyday goods, and the National Basketball Association solves the problem of people wanting world-class sports entertainment. Every single business – big and small – solves a problem.

Lumped into the focus area of "solving a problem" is building a world-class solution that fits your customers' needs. Part of solving a problem also involves providing customer support for people who are using your solution, but the core part of this is your **offering**. The NBA focuses on the quality of the play around the league when it comes to solving the problem of basketball fans wanting a world-class sports entertainment experience, but that also means that they need to focus on their distribution channels (TV deals, radio deals, advertising deals to make sure fans know about exciting upcoming games, etc.).

To apply it to your business, here's what you need to focus on when it comes to solving a problem for your customers:

1) What problem(s) does your business solve for your customers?

2) How do you provide a world-class solution to that problem? What is your product/service? How do you make them enjoy that solution and get results from that solution? How can you make your product/service the best in the business?

3) What is the customer's experience with your solution – from start to finish? How do they engage with your company, how does the solution get delivered, and who do they turn to if they are having problems with the solution?

Once you've figured out what problem your business solves, your next focus is to **find leads**, or find people who are interested in paying money for your solution. Most business classes and business books make this activity seem challenging, but it's actually quite simple. In fact, to find leads for your business, there's only two questions you need to answer:

1) Who would benefit from my solution?

2) Where are those people?

The "who would benefit from my solution?" should be easy to answer if you've done the work to identify your customer avatar from earlier in this chapter. Your customer avatar is the person who would benefit most from the solution that you are offering.

As far as "where are those people?", you need to consider where you can find people like your customer avatar. Where does he/she hang out online? Where does he/she spend his/her time in person? Do they go to networking events like the Chamber of Commerce? Are they attending industry conferences and seminars? Do they frequently visit certain websites or blogs on the internet? Do they post in certain internet forums? Are they active in certain Facebook groups?

By knowing the answers to these questions, you'll know exactly where you need to be in order to meet your ideal customers. For example, if you're a mortgage broker, then your ideal customer is someone who is buying a house. Where do those people spend their time? Well, it's obvious... they spend a lot of time with their real estate agent looking at houses!

In order to find those types of leads, why not befriend local real estate agents and establish relationships with them so that you can get referrals from them? That's an excellent way to find potential customers for your mortgage broker business.

Or, let's pretend that you're an accountant who specializes in tax returns for sole proprietorships. Your ideal customer is clearly small business owners. Rather than leaving a stack of business cards in a coffee shop (which is a silly tactic that most newpreneurs use... take a second to consider who is in the coffee shop; the percent of coffee shop-goers who are also small business owners is very small!), it would be far more fruitful to attend Chamber of Commerce events, where over 90% of attendees are small business owners.

Think about **where** your ideal customers are, and you need to be there. If your solution is for something that's not so obvious, you can always consider the online activities of your ideal customers.

For example, let's say you want to start a travel agency that helps people plan adventure trips to Costa Rica. I highly doubt there's a physical gathering in your area of people who are trying to plan adventure trips to Costa Rica, but I do know for a fact that there are thousands of people who are searching for this on Google.

For your sake, to illustrate this example, I've used Google's Keyword Research Tool to see how many people search for "Costa Rica zip" or similar terms. It came up with 12 suggested search terms, including "Costa Rica zip line," "Costa Rica ziplining," "Costa Rica zip line tours," etc. According to Google's own research tool, 2,170 people from around the United States search for these terms every single month.

Google charges on average $1.07 for each click if you advertise for these search terms, which means that if you had $100 to spend on advertising to these people, you'd get around 93 clicks to your website. If your business offers to solve this problem by charging people $100 to plan their Costa Rican ziplining tour, then all you'd need is 1 out of every 93 clicks to convert into becoming a customer for you to be profitable.

By advertising where your ideal customers are (in this case, your ideal customers are on Google searching for "Costa Rica ziplining"), you are getting in front of targeted leads that could become your customers. Using the above real life numbers, if you could get 5 people out of your 93 clicks to buy your service for $100, you'd generate $500 in revenue off of just $100 in advertising on Google. Remember – these leads are highly targeted, since you know for a fact that they were searching for "Costa Rica ziplining" on Google.

...isn't that a much more targeted approach than

leaving your business cards in random places?

Of course, the above example assumes that you have a process in place that **turns leads into customers**, which is the third area of focus for you as an entrepreneur. Once you've decided on the problem that you're solving and you've determined where your ideal customers are, you need to establish processes that convert those people into paying customers.

When I launched NewGen Consultants, an internet marketing agency, in 2012, my business partner and I decided that local small businesses were our ideal customers. So, one day when we were vetting our idea out to see if it could become a feasible business, we decided to walk in to a local sandwich shop and pitch our marketing services to the owner.

After an improvised sales pitch, the business owner said something we weren't expecting... "Sure, what are the next steps?"

Admittedly, we had no clue what the next steps were, as we hadn't focused on how we turn leads into paying customers. We knew what the problem was (small businesses don't get as many customers as they'd like), we knew **where** our ideal customers were (at their small business locations within our hometown), but we hadn't at all focused on how we'd **turn those leads into customers** (all we had was an improvised sales pitch that we hoped would do the trick).

Rather than spending time on non-essential tasks like a logo, a website, a business plan, etc., we would have benefited far more if we had established an onboarding process for new clients. In the end, we asked the business owner to write us a check and let him know that we'd be in touch, but in hindsight we should have been far more organized.

New entrepreneurs **must** focus on having processes

that not only turn leads into customers, but they need to spend time knowing what will happen next for their new customers. Fast forward a few months, and the NewGen process was far more refined: we sent leads a free report detailing how we could improve their website's Search Engine Optimization, we then sent them a detailed proposal that included a button for payment, and once they paid we sent them an onboarding document that detailed what we needed from them, as well as what the next steps were.

Building a process that turns leads into customers is different depending on what type of business you are running, but typically it involves some of the following activities:

1) How you pitch or offer your product/service to the lead. This can be an in-person pitch, an online pitch (such as a webpage that lays out your offer and its features and benefits), an email pitch, or a telephone pitch.

2) How you accept payment. Do you require up-front payment? Partial up-front payment? Are there are any future fees? If you don't take payment today, what are the terms of future payments? Do you automatically charge their credit card?

3) What are the next steps once they become your customer? Do you need anything from the customer? Can you fulfill the order right away? What's the expected timeline?

By focusing on these three tasks (which problem you'll solve and **how**, finding leads, and turning leads into customers), you'll be focusing on the true **profit-generating** activities. Getting a logo, enhancing your website, hiring a virtual assistant, and other activities are nice, but none of them will really move your business forward as far as your bottom line is concerned.

The key here is to **FOCUS** on the activities that will actually make your business profitable and sustainable.

Shiny Object Syndrome

No book on focusing as an entrepreneur would be complete without mentioning the "shiny object syndrome" and information overload. These are two of the biggest enemies to entrepreneurs, as they're so effective at distracting us from growing our businesses.

If you've never heard of it before, "shiny object syndrome" is where a new strategy, tip, tactic, or tool turns your head and makes you put your revenue-generating activities to the side in order to pursue this new "shiny object."

The most common "shiny object" that I've seen distract entrepreneurs is new tools. For example, almost every entrepreneur has a to-do list. Historically, to-do lists were hand-written on a piece of paper, but with the advent of technology and the internet we've seen to-do lists shift to more technologically-advanced lists. Some people use their iPhone Reminders app as their to-do list, some use Evernote, and some people still stick to good old-fashioned pieces of paper.

Now, though, there is seemingly a new to-do tool on the market every week. Asana has become the most widely used to-do list tool on the internet, but newcomers such as Wunderlist, Any.Do, and Todoist have all come onto the scene in recent years and months. For some reason, these new tools always seem to turn heads, and too many entrepreneurs fall for this trap and spend time testing these new tools out. The old saying of "if it's not broken, don't fix it" comes to mind, but with so many shiny objects on the marketplace it's hard to resist the urge.

Communication tools are another example of potential shiny objects. Whereas almost everyone on the internet uses email as their primary source of communication, new communication tools such as Slack have proven to be shiny objects. Admittedly, I've fallen victim to Slack, and have spent countless hours trying to get my team, clients, and vendors to use this new collaboration and communication tool. In the end, I realized it was a waste of my time, and went back to focusing on the three things that would actually grow my business (my solutions/offerings, finding leads, and turning those leads into customers).

The invisible shiny objects are new strategies that people chase. As a new entrepreneur, be wary of "new" strategies that people tell you to chase. For example, if you're a graphic designer, and some other graphic designer tells you that they've received a lot of business from Craigslist, don't totally change your direction and put all of your eggs into the Craigslist basket. For one, what works for someone else isn't guaranteed to work for you, and second, if you're already focused on a different medium, remain focused.

If you are constantly changing directions, you'll be starting from scratch each and every time, and your results will prove that. One common theme that I see for people who are growing online businesses is that they are constantly changing mediums. I've seen newpreneurs "try" Facebook, "try" Twitter, "try" Instagram, and "try" Pinterest. They constantly hear about people succeeding on each of those platforms, and then they wonder why they're not enjoying similar successes.

This brings up a few points. First of all, if you constantly jump from one platform to another, you're going up against people who have put all of their eggs into one basket and **FOCUS**ed (remember, Follow One Course Until Success). If you only "try" Facebook for a few weeks or months and then give up in order to "try" a different platform, how do you expect to compete against people who have spent years truly mastering Facebook?

If you're the person who jumps from one strategy to another, you're essentially a woodpecker that's pecking ten times on 1,000 different trees. If there's a woodpecker out there that instead pecks 10,000 times on just one tree, guess who's going to get better results.

Secondly, and most importantly, we need to address the term "try." I've never seen Star Wars, but the Yoda quote of "Do or do not, there is no try" has been a cornerstone of entrepreneurial success not only for me, but for entrepreneurs in all industries. Too many entrepreneurs say that they've "tried" something, when in fact there's no such thing as "trying."

I've best seen this illustrated with a practical example. Right now, *try* to physically put this book down. Now, either one of two things happened: either you put the book down, or you didn't. There's no such thing as you "trying" to put the book down… you either did, or didn't.

The same rings true for entrepreneurs. It's not possible to "try" succeeding with Facebook Ads. Either you succeeded with them, or you didn't. The "easy" reply to my argument is to say "Ok, well I *tried*, but they didn't work."

Please remember this for every aspect of your business – and personal – life: If you *tried* something and it didn't work for you, but it's worked for other people, then it's not the *thing* that didn't work… it's *you*. If you tried Facebook Ads and they didn't work, but you know they've worked for others, then it's not Facebook Ads that don't work. Indeed, it's you. You haven't mastered them enough, you didn't give them the chance to succeed, or you just weren't creative enough to find a new way to get them to work. It's never the medium that "doesn't work."

Above all else, the most dangerous "shiny object" for

newpreneurs is alternative revenue streams. When you start a business, the first few months – and likely the first year – can be a struggle. It takes some time to get into the groove of being your own boss, and it certainly takes time to start building up your business's revenue. While this is happening, it's inevitable that you'll come across different revenue streams that other people are using to make money, particularly online.

If you're setting out to become a photographer or web designer or graphic designer, or **any** other business, it's easy to fall into the trap of looking at the latest and greatest ways of making money online and thinking that you'll do that "on the side" while you build your main business's revenue up.

In the most extreme example I can think of, one of my students who was building a photography business decided that it would be "easy" to make money by selling soap. Yes, soap. When I asked him why he got that idea rather than focusing on finding more clients for his photography business, he suggested that he uses soap, so he knows a lot about it, and that he read it's easy to create your own soap.

Let's for a second pretend that it *is* indeed easy to make money selling soap. Had this student gone down that path, there is little to no chance that his photography business would have grown. An old Chinese proverb says that "a man who chases two rabbits catches neither," and that's especially true for entrepreneurs.

If you truly want to succeed with the business that you're starting, you need to become **absolutely obsessed** with succeeding with that business. To take it even one step further, **success needs to be the only option**, which means that making money "on the side" with a totally different business shouldn't be an option, and nor should having a backup plan. When success is the **only** option, you will succeed.

One of the key contributors to my business partner and I going separate ways with our Search Engine Optimization agency is that he always had a fall-back plan. Knowing that his life partner would be relocated in two years due to her career path, my business partner always talked about where he'd be... and our business seemingly never factored into that view of the future. He also had going back into corporate America and potentially earning his master's degree in the back of his mind, so it came as no surprise to me when he finally threw the towel in on being an entrepreneur.

All of this leads to one of the most common questions that I'm asked: "Brian, is it possible to start a business while working a full-time job?"

The answer is yes. And there's even a term for that... it's called a "side hustle."

Like I said earlier about Facebook Ads "not working," it's impossible for me to say that *anything* couldn't work. Indeed, you have the power to make *any* situation or circumstance work out (and don't ever let anyone tell you otherwise!). When I started NewGen Consultants in 2012, I spent six months in my corporate job while laying the groundwork for NewGen.

With that said, though, I now look back on those six months and realize that I was churning my wheels with no results during that time. My business partner and I were both working 40 hours per week in our "day jobs," and then meeting at night to discuss how we would grow NewGen Consultants. If you've learned anything from me by now, you'd know that this was *not* an efficient use of our time; instead, we should have been focusing on the three revenue-generating activities of 1) building out our solutions, 2) findings leads, and 3) turning those leads into customers.

It's definitely possible to use a day job as a safety net, but it's always been my belief that it's far easier to succeed without the comfort of a 9 to 5. When your back is up against the wall then you're forced to take action, and at the end of the day it's action that breeds success.

There is one caveat, though. If you don't have *any* money saved up, then it could be premature to leave your job. When you're strapped for cash and aren't even sure if you can cover your next month's bills, then you'll be forced to make business decisions based on immediate revenue, which doesn't bode well for your business's long-term health. Every great entrepreneur is in a position to make decisions based on the long-term well-being of their company and their customers or clients, and if leaving your job strips you from being in that position then it's premature to leave.

The final "shiny object" is information. Information overload plagues every entrepreneur, because it's so addicting to learn more and read more about how you can grow your business. There's so much information available to us on the internet, on podcasts, on television, and in magazines, which makes it hard to avoid information.

I've enjoyed the biggest successes in my entrepreneurial life when I've completely avoided new information. For a long time I was constantly flooding my brain with case studies, buying online courses, and reading every article online about entrepreneurship and growing a business, and sooner or later it hit me that I was on the hunt for some sort of golden nugget that would propel my business past the $1 million mark.

I became **obsessed** with reading and consuming every bit of information in search of that elusive one golden nugget... the *one* piece of information that would reveal a strategy or tactic that could change my entire future.

What I realized was that that golden nugget doesn't

really exist. Sooner or later I realized that none of the information I was reading or listening to was new, and I already knew all of the content I was consuming.

In the world of Facebook newsfeeds and Twitter timelines it's easy to click link after link, but what I'm asking you to do is **avoid information**. I promise you that you have all of the information you need in order to start your business, and if you don't then you'll quickly gain that information by just *taking action* in your business.

Because of this advice, you may be wondering if you should continue reading at this point. If you stop right here and never read a single page more because you're too busy taking action, then I don't blame you. But if you want to gain my nearly ten years of experience in building multiple successful businesses, working with dozens of clients from around the United States, and working with thousands of students from around the world, then I promise you that the information contained in the following pages is well worth your time… it just won't contain that *one golden nugget*.

As you know by now, this book is full of useful entrepreneurial teachings, mainly illustrated by anecdotes of my own and of others. Within these anecdotes are nuggets of knowledge that should help frame your entrepreneurial mindset for success.

Become Obsessed

When I talk about the need for newpreneurs to focus, what I really want to convey is that new entrepreneurs need to become **absolutely obsessed** about their business and **absolutely obsessed** about success.

Becoming obsessed means different things to different people, but for a start, you need to get in the habit of doing at least one thing per day that moves your business forward. No matter what your situation is – whether you have a full-time job or not – you need to commit to doing one thing per day that moves you closer to your goals.

When I say "one thing per day," that means each and every day. In case you need a reminder, there are seven days in a week – not five. Mark Cuban, the famous billionaire owner of the Dallas Mavericks, and one of the most well-known sharks on ABC's show *Shark Tank*, always says that entrepreneurs need to work as if there's someone out there working 24 hours a day to take it all away from you… because there is.

If you choose to take a day off, or if you only work five days a week, then I *promise* you that there's someone like me out there who is working harder than you in order to be more successful than you. One of the keys to my success – particularly with Premiership Talk – has been working harder than anyone else out there. To those that are thinking "why work harder when I can work smarter?" – my answer is that I work harder *and* smarter. You need to as well.

When you get into the habit of doing at least one action per day that moves your business forward, before long you'll become obsessed with your business and your success. You won't care about missing a party with your friends. I promise you that there will be more parties, and that if you put the work in today then your parties of tomorrow will be far more fun, in far more appealing locations, and with many more people who care about you and who you care about. (Look up Awesomeness Fest – there are thousands of applicants per year, and I was accepted and attended my first one in October 2015. We all got there by working harder and smarter over the course of our lives, and all of the parties and events that we missed can't even compare to the insanity of letting loose in exotic locations like Costa Rica and Mexico).

When you become obsessed with your business, you think about it night and day. You talk to people around you about it. You don't think about the hours that you're putting in, and instead think about the results that you're getting. When you become obsessed, it's all you want to do. Living a mediocre and unfulfilled life doesn't even seem like an option anymore, and you make a firm commitment to yourself to never be average again.

When I was still working 40 hours per week at my day job, I was getting home at 5:30pm each night. I'd eat dinner, relax for half an hour, and then hustle until 2am each night. I was only getting five hours of sleep each night, but it didn't bother me because I wanted to succeed more than I wanted to sleep. I spent weekends working on my businesses, because I wanted to succeed more than I wanted to watch TV and hang out with friends. **Do you want to succeed more than you want to watch Breaking Bad?**

Become obsessed with your business, and you'll automatically be on the right path to success. It starts with just taking one action per day to move your business forward.

4

The Only Way You'll Get Stuff Done: Productivity

Success as an entrepreneur ultimately hinges on one thing: how productive you are. The smartest person in the world would die a poor and unknown man/woman if they weren't productive and never took any action. Talent or knowledge means nothing without action, so productivity is the cornerstone of success.

Of course, this chapter on productivity could be as simple as saying "**get stuff done**," but the fact of the matter is that it's not that simple. As an entrepreneur, there are a million reasons why you'll have times when you don't get stuff done so easily, and in my years of starting and running businesses I've learned some productivity hacks that help me power through anything standing in my way.

First things first, as an entrepreneur it's imperative that you understand the difference between **action** and **motion**. The difference between these two ultimately determines what results you actually get and what you actually get done, versus what you just spend your time on without getting any results.

James Clear (of jamesclear.com) describes the difference between these two concepts best. "Motion is when you're busy doing something, but that task will never produce an outcome by itself," James wrote on his blog. "Action, on the other hand, is the type of behavior that will get you a result."

To give some examples, if you're trying to lose weight and you research diets, call the gym and ask for a personal trainer, and watch the *Food Network* to see how to cook healthy meals, those activities are all just **motion**. To take **action**, you'd need to go on a run, lift weights, or eat salad for lunch every day for a month.

To use an entrepreneurial example, when it comes to growing your online business, **motion** would be replying to emails, creating an outline for your next product offering, or reading articles online about how to find more customers for your business. **Action** would be picking up the phone and closing deals with your current prospects, actually building out your next product offering, or completing work on a current client project.

The dangerous part of to-do lists is that they're often full of **motion** activities, and very little **action** activities. The danger with **motion** is that it makes us *feel* busy – because we are, after all, doing things! – but those activities don't yield results. You can do all the research in the world about how to find more customers for your business, but that will **never** actually get you more customers. That's motion. Picking up the phone and pitching someone, however, **will** get you more clients. That's action.

Let's look at a typical newpreneur's to-do list. Keep in mind, for a new entrepreneur, there's really only **one** goal: get your first paying customer. That's it. Everything else is secondary in the beginning. But here's what a typical to-do list looks like…

1) Decide on a company name

2) Create website

3) Get a logo

4) Create a Facebook page

5) Create a Twitter profile

6) Create a LinkedIn page

7) Share it with friends and family

Hopefully by now you can identify that **all of the above activities** are motion activities. Creating your website won't get you your first paying customer. Neither will getting a logo. Nor will creating a Facebook page or other social media profiles. Instead, the **one thing** that will get you your first paying customer is **talking to potential customers**, and closing one of them into a sale. That's it. The rest of your to-do list will keep you busy, that's for sure, but it will *not* help you achieve your goal.

James speculates that we choose motion over action because motion makes us *feel* like we're making progress, without any risk of failure or criticism. For example, if you're trying to lose weight, then you might look dumb trying to use the exercise machines. So as James points out on his website, you just talk to the trainer about their rates instead. Another prime example from his website deals directly with entrepreneurs: "Yes, I'd like to land more clients for my business. But, if I ask for the sale, I might get turned down. So maybe I should just email 10 potential clients instead."

All of this leads me to two important points that I've learned when it comes to productivity. The first point is that you need to **decide the one thing you are trying to accomplish**. At any given moment in time, what I'm trying to accomplish can change. For example, as of this exact moment (when I'm writing this), my goal is to finish writing this book. Once I've decided that that's what I'm trying to accomplish, the second point is that I need to decide what **action** will help me accomplish that. In this case, I need to write. Nothing else that I can do qualifies as action; it's all motion.

If rather than writing I decide to work on my outline for the book, then that's motion. All the outlining and planning in the world won't get the book done. If I decide to think of a name for the book, that's motion. If I start working on the cover for the book, that's motion. The *only* action that I need to take is to **write**. Keep this in mind as you work to launch and grow your business.

You may have noticed that I said you need to decide what the **one thing** that you want to accomplish is. This approach to productivity is a newer one for me, but it has transformed my results in life and in business. Rather than having an extensive to-do list of a million things that I need to do, at any given moment in time I focus on **one thing** that I want to accomplish, and my entire to-do list is comprised of just the **action activity** that can make that one thing happen.

With that said, I actually have a few "one things." But – they always focus on different areas of my life. For example, when it comes to my business, I only allow myself to have **one** "one thing" that I'm focusing on. Of course, my business is multi-faceted, but I still only focus on one thing at a time.

For example, my business is made up of online courses that I sell, speaking engagements around the United States, a very select group of private clients, and other programs that I run (such as my Inner Circle group). At any given moment in time, I know that I can't possibly push all of those different fronts forward, so I focus on one at a time. My focus might shift daily, it might shift weekly, or I might be in the middle of a busy time and need to shift my focus midway through the day. But no matter what, I have **one** focus at a time, and my to-do list is made up **only** of the **one** activity that will help me accomplish that goal.

At the same time, I allow myself to have one health goal. For example, I make sure that I do *something* active each and every day. Some days that means I go kayaking in the middle of the day, some days it means I hit the gym, some days it means I go for a swim, but I let health be its own "thing" that gets my attention every day.

The third "one thing" that is on my list every day is relationships. Every single day I make it a point to connect to *someone*. Of course, I talk to my closest friends and my family every day, but at least once per day I reach out to a friend, a fellow entrepreneur, or just someone who I haven't talked to in ages.

So, at any moment in time, I have three "one things:" one thing that I'm trying to accomplish for my business (and the **one** activity that will get me there), one activity for the day that concerns my health and well-being, and one person who I'm going to reach out to and connect with, either online or in person.

If I wasn't honest with myself and allowed myself to focus on booking speaking gigs, landing podcast interviews, creating a new course or program, and writing a book, then chances are I'd get overwhelmed and not take any action at all. Simply managing all of those things at once involves a lot of **motion** rather than action, so instead I just focus on one thing at a time.

My college self would have laughed at the concept of the **one thing**, as I always prided myself on "multi-tasking." The fact of the matter is, though, that multi-tasking doesn't exist. For example, I know a lot of people who believe they can watch TV and work at the same time. It's impossible. Either you're working, or you're watching TV. It's one or the other, but never both. Try watching TV right now while reading this book... you'll notice that you can't do both at the same time. Multi-tasking does not exist. (Except, of course, chewing gum and walking... I have faith that you *can* do that at the same time!)

You can extrapolate this concept into the work that you do as well. For example, most people kid themselves and say that they'll multi-task as they respond to emails. Again, you're either responding to emails, or you're doing your work... never both. For this reason, I have completely stopped letting emails and social media notifications run my day. Instead, I'll happily ignore emails while I'm working, and then will set aside dedicated times when I go back and respond to everything in my inbox and in my social media accounts.

The problem with going back and forth between your work and these other distractions is that the time spent switching gears between the two causes you to lose a lot of productivity. The best illustration I've seen of this is a very simple activity that you can do at home, right now. All you need is a piece of paper, a pen, and a stopwatch (your smartphone is probably the best option!).

Start the stopwatch on your smartphone, and on the piece of paper, write out the alphabet on one line, and the numbers 1 through 26 on the line below the alphabet. Do it as fast as you can. Again – write the alphabet on the top line, and as soon as you finish, write out the numbers 1 through 26 on the second line.

How long did it take? If you didn't do it, take the time to actually do it... I promise it will forever change the way you look at "multi-tasking."

Okay, so if the above activity took you 30 seconds, set a *timer* this time for 30 seconds, **NOT** the stopwatch. Now you only have 30 seconds (or however long the first activity took you) to complete this next task.

When you start the timer, you're going to do the exact same activity as before, but **write one letter out, and then one number, and then the next letter, and then the next number,** and so on. So for example, once the timer starts, write A on the top line, and then write 1 on the second line. Then write B on the top line, and then write 2 on the second line. Go all the way from A to Z, alternating between writing a letter and a number each time.

How far did you get within the allotted time? You had the **exact amount of time** that it took you to complete the task when you were focused on one thing at a time (letters vs. numbers), but chances are you didn't finish when you were multi-tasking and alternating between writing letters and numbers. I'm also willing to bet that your work was lower quality (your handwriting was probably sloppier this time around!), and you may have even made a mistake.

...so that's why I no longer believe in multi-tasking. As simple as the task may seem – even as simple as writing out the alphabet and counting to 26 – your brain isn't optimized to alternate between two tasks. Stick to **one thing**, and your work will not only be more efficient (meaning you get more done in less time), but it will be higher quality. Who doesn't like better quality work, with more production, in less time? That's a productivity hack!

At this point, in just a few pages, you've already learned the difference of motion and action, you've seen the power of the **one thing**, and we've busted the myth of multi-tasking. The next biggest tool in my productivity arsenal is **reverse-engineering**. When it comes to productivity, I *love* breaking things down and reverse-engineering what I need to do in order to accomplish my biggest goals.

I've always looked up to Stephen King as an example of how powerful reverse engineering is. I've never read his books, but King is one of the highest-paid writers of all time. According to *Forbes*, this is a guy who has made $45 million in a single year, just through writing books, and some sources list his estimated net worth in excess of $400 million. King has published over 50 novels, with each and every one of them being classified as a best-seller. Publishing over **50 novels** is no small feat, and shows that King has mastered the art of being productive and taking action. Those books didn't write themselves, after all!

To complete the monumental task of writing a novel, Stephen King breaks each novel down to its most basic form. A novel is nothing more than 180,000 words. So, rather than worrying about how he's going to write 180,000 words, he simply writes 2,000 words per day. I don't know how long that takes him, but for me, that's about two hours of writing. After doing that for just three months, he has a completed novel. How much easier is that than worrying about the huge task of writing 180,000 words? By breaking it down, the smaller tasks are easier and more attainable, and add up over time.

To bring this into entrepreneurial terms, when I started making money on my soccer website, Premiership Talk, I knew I wanted to break the milestone of 100,000 visitors per month. When I sat down and asked myself how I would possibly hit 100,000 visitors per month, it seemed like a huge task. So instead of worrying about such a big number, I reverse engineered it.

In order to get 100,000 visitors per month, I'd need to get 25,000 visitors each week. In order to do that, I'd need to get 3,571 visitors per day. Answering the question of "how can I get 3,571 visitors per day?" is much easier than answering the question of "where will I find 100,000 visitors per month?"

When I reverse-engineered it further, I knew that my average post at the time got around 500 visitors. So, in order to get 3,571 visitors per day, I'd need to publish at least seven articles. No problem! Each article only took about 20 minutes to write, so I was looking at about three hours of work in order to publish seven articles, which would attract 3,600 visitors, which would lead to 100,000 visitors per month. Check that out! Over time I got smarter about asking different questions (such as "how can I get more visitors per post?"), but at the beginning it paid to just put the work in to get the site to grow.

You can apply this concept to your business in many ways. First of all, if you have a revenue target you can break it down further to see what's required to hit that goal. Most new entrepreneurs always target $100,000 as their first major revenue goal. If you break that down, that's $8,333 per month, or $2,083 per week. That might sound like a lot – as most people can't relate to making over $2,000 each and every week – but there are other ways to reverse engineer your targets. For example, if you're a web designer and you sell websites at $3,000, then you only need to sell three websites per month to make $100,000 (three websites per month at $3,000 equals $9,000 per month, which adds up to $108,000). Rather than reverse engineering by time, you can always divide your revenue goal by your revenue per deal, and divide the two in order to see how many deals you need to make in order to hit that goal. Then, figure out how many deals you need to close on per month and per week.

By doing this, you'll have clear goals each week. If we continue using the above example of a web designer who needs to make three website deals per month, then each week that web designer needs to set out with the intention of closing just **one** website deal per week. Anything else, and he/she will be ahead of schedule, and will allow some leeway in the event that they can't close a deal on a certain week (or, they can surpass their initial goal!).

Whatever your goal is, make sure you reverse engineer it, and let that drive your intentions and actions.

Just-in-Time Learning

I'm not going to call out any one of my 3,000+ students in this chapter, because nearly *every single one of them* is guilty of this next productivity-killer. Of course, this problem goes far beyond my students, and is the most common productivity-killer for almost all entrepreneurs.

That productivity-killer is **learning**. As entrepreneurs, we all love to learn. The internet makes it so easy to learn new things; YouTube, Facebook, blogs, and news articles all can teach us new things, and pretty much any information is now available at our fingertips thanks to Google.

Whenever I check in with my students, I always ask "what did you do today?" to see if they're making strides each and every day. To their credit, they often have their businesses on their mind, but to their discredit, they often waste countless hours learning, watching instructional videos, reading blog articles, and watching educational YouTube videos.

Learning feels good because it feels productive. It feels like you're moving forward and gaining knowledge that you'll need at some point. It's easy to justify learning by convincing yourself that it's saving you time in the future.

The reality is that learning is **motion**. Learning how to get more customers won't get you more customers.

Of course, the most obvious argument to my point here is that you'll never be able to do something if you don't *learn* how to do it first.

Fine. I'll give you that. But that's where I've come up with the concept of *just-in-time learning*. In manufacturing, there's a concept known as *just-in-time inventory*. Using this approach, manufacturing companies only produce their goods as orders come in so that they don't have excess inventory just laying around the warehouse. If there are only orders for 100 items, they'll manufacture 100 items (*maybe* they'll manufacture 125 just to be safe, but they certainly won't manufacture 500 items, as that would take up valuable shelf space).

When you start a business and spend your days learning about marketing, learning about graphic design, learning about public speaking, learning about generating website traffic, learning about social media strategies, learning about copywriting, etc., then you're building up an excess of knowledge. The worst part about that is that by the time you ever need those things, you'll need a refresher because all of that knowledge won't stick.

Instead, as a new entrepreneur, you'll benefit immensely by implementing *just-in-time learning*. Along the lines of the "one thing" that we discussed above – decide what the **one thing** you want to accomplish is (such as "getting my first customer"), and then *only* learn what is absolutely essential to accomplish that one goal. That's just-in-time learning in action. Learn things "just in time" – not far ahead of time and long before you ever need that knowledge.

Plan Ahead

This last productivity tip is simple yet effective: plan ahead. When deciding to write this book, the best advice I received was "don't stop writing until you know what's next." Long before I heard that advice in the context of writing a book, I've practiced that for most of my life. This productivity tip is literally as simple as planning out your tomorrow at the end of today.

If you plan your tomorrow at the end of today, then you'll be able to hit the ground running in the morning. I love combining this productivity hack with batch processing, and I actually structure my weeks out based on batching. For example, on Mondays I typically do any video filming that I need with my videographer, on Tuesdays I work on my products and programs (as well as building out new products), on Wednesdays I work on my autoresponder sequences (the email series that my leads and customers go through) and advertising campaigns, on Thursdays I typically do my media appearances (podcasts, being interviewed for blogs, etc.), and on Fridays I typically do my outreach to potential partners, fellow entrepreneurs in my various networking groups and masterminds, and friends that I want to check in on.

By having a system in place like this, I am immediately productive when I sit down to work each day. I know exactly what I'm doing, and because I'm not wasting time alternating between tasks, I get the most done in the shortest amount of time possible, allowing me to also exercise each day and feel good.

If you're stuck in a full-time job (like I was for a while), that's not an excuse to not be productive. In fact, in this case it's even *more* important that your weeks are structured, and you'll probably want to be even more specific with regards to times that you'll do activities. For example, if you know that you get home from work at 5:30pm every night, then give yourself an hour for dinner, cleaning the dishes, and changing out of your work clothes, and then work from 7pm to 10pm every night. That's three hours right there.

…and if you want to accelerate your results, give up a little bit of sleep and work until midnight, which will give you **five hours** of week each night, even after working at your full-time job. Five hours per night is 25 hours during the week, plus any time that you work on your business during the weekend… there's no reason you can't make it work with that much time on your hands!

And always remember – when you're forgoing sleep and other fun activities, it's temporary. You always need to ask yourself if you're willing to temporarily miss out on those things in order to obtain long-term success. For me, the answer was always yes. For every other successful entrepreneur, the answer was always yes.

In this chapter you've learned some of my productivity strategies, techniques, and hacks. The important thing is that you decide what works for you and decide what strategies help you get the most done. But – above all else – make sure you **take action** and avoid motion whenever possible, and make sure that you never get distracted from whatever your *one goal* is. If you are just starting your business and you don't have any revenue yet, every task that you do must be geared towards getting your first paying client or customer; nothing else matters at the beginning.

5

Standing Out in a Crowded World: Excellence

This is without a doubt going to be the shortest chapter in the book, because it's something that comes naturally when you're in the right mindset and when you've completely committed to being successful.

But, nonetheless, the topic is important enough that I wanted to include just a couple of pages about **excellence**. "Excellence" means a lot of different things to different people, but when it comes to entrepreneurship, you need to expect, demand, and strive for excellence in every single thing that you do.

As an entrepreneur, you're no longer an employee of a company – you **are** the company. As such, every thing that **you** do reflects on your company. You and your company are one in the same.

On that note, one of the best pieces of advice I've ever received is from Suzanne Evans, one of the most successful business coaches in the world. Suzanne went from being a secretary in New York City, living poor and struggling to pay rent, to running a multi-million dollar coaching business. She is a best-selling author and hosts one of the biggest and most extravagant business conferences of the year, with 1,000 influential business owners in attendance annually.

Suzanne's most consistent message – and the topic of one of her books – is "how you do anything is how you do everything." Suzanne argues that however you do *anything* in your life is indicative of how you do *everything*. If you don't care about the little things, then you don't care enough about the big things. If you're okay with sloppy work on certain tasks because it "doesn't matter," then that same carelessness will creep into your more important tasks. How you do anything is how you do everything.

I've worked with thousands of students from around the world, and I always know who the successful ones will be by how they complete the smaller, less important assignments. The amount of effort that they put into those are indicative of how much they care and how much they're committed to their success, and I'm rarely wrong when I guess based on these seemingly smaller tasks.

Similarly, when I'm working with freelancers and service providers, I always look at the tiny things in their work. Are there little spelling mistakes in their proposals? Is the formatting a bit off on their website? Is the year in the copyright at the bottom of their website updated? Do they always capitalize the name of their company appropriately? Are their emails written correctly? These things seem small, but paying attention to them has saved me tens of thousands of dollars in mistakes by not working with companies that don't show excellence in *everything* they do.

A former business partner of mine had less than impressive attention to detail. I was wary about this when we started our business together, and in hindsight I was blinded by our friendship and overlooked the clues in all of the little details. About a year into our partnership, I was on vacation in the Dominican Republic while he was getting flyers printed for an upcoming event we were hosting in New York City. When I arrived back in Boston and saw a sample of the flyers on my desk, I was horrified to see that our company name was spelled wrong (two of the letters were swapped around).

My business partner insisted that it was fine and not worth printing an entirely new batch for just two swapped letters, and that told me everything I needed to know… chances are his work elsewhere was riddled with tiny errors. It's these tiny errors that can one day lead to bigger errors, and indeed they did over time. Our clients started picking up on these small errors (like their addresses being listed incorrectly on websites), which caused more headaches and re-work than I'd care to remember.

How you do anything is how you do everything. Take pride in the little things, and people will notice. When I was hosting the 2015 IM Summit, a virtual conference attended by over 1,400 entrepreneurs featuring some of the world's top speakers and entrepreneurs, I made sure to do all the little things extremely well since I wanted to build deep relationships with the incredible speakers.

Once I had the speaker lineup arranged, I had to follow up with each of the speakers individually to book their interview times. Rather than just typing out an email – which certainly would have sufficed – I decided to shoot 15 personalized videos, one for each speaker. These videos were only about two minutes in length, where I thanked the speaker for agreeing to participate and gave them all of the relevant information they needed to know.

Nonetheless, that tiny small bit of work and personalization went a long way, with almost every speaker emailing me back to say that they appreciated the video. One of them even called me to say that it was a nice touch, and asked me how I always think of the little things that make them feel special.

There's no good way to answer that question, but at the core of my success over time has been due to raising my standards. Of course, when I started my first business, it was just a blog, and I had no long-term vision or plans for it. My "standards" were really non-existent. I just woke up, blogged, and tried to make improvements here and there.

What really raised my standards with Premiership Talk was when I heard about the success of other bloggers. Once I knew how much money they were making from advertising deals, I started dissecting their businesses, and could see that the standards they set were extremely high. All of the little things were to a much higher standard than what I was used to. Their logos were designed by graphic designers, the fonts used on their website were consistent and user-friendly, and all of their posts were of the highest quality. What I quickly realized was that in order to achieve the success that they enjoyed, I'd need to raise my standards to be as good – or better – than them.

Tony Robbins says it best. "Any time you sincerely want to make a change, the first thing you must do is to raise your standards," he wrote in his book *Awaken the Giant Within*. "When people ask me what really changed my life eight years ago, I tell them that absolutely the most important thing was changing what I demanded of myself. I wrote down all the things I would no longer accept in my life, all the things I would no longer tolerate, and all the things that I aspired to becoming."

The reason why this excerpt resonates with me is that Tony discusses how raising your standards not only involves elevating your game, but also cutting out aspects of your business and of your life that you no longer want to accept. Are you guilty of sometimes slacking off? Do you delay your success by wasting countless hours on Facebook? Do you swear and act unprofessional at times? Do you save things for "tomorrow"? Do you eat unhealthy, causing you to not be at your best? Do you get too little sleep? These are things that may be plaguing you and lowering your standards, and it's time to cut them out.

The final point I want to raise while we're talking about excellence is being different. Seth Godin, who famously disapproves of the modern standardized American education system, once said that "the reason they want you to fit in is that once you do, they can ignore you." It's easy to ignore businesses (and people) that are just like everyone else. It's easy to overlook Sal's Ice Cream Parlor when their ice cream is just like every other ice cream place within a 50 mile radius.

It's not so easy, though, to ignore places that do things differently. In my own local region, a new "microcreamery" opened up, where they create small and very different batches of ice cream, such as apple pie ice cream that literally has pieces of apple pie in it — apples and pie crust included! Whereas most ice cream places flounder as the winter months approach, the microcreamery is flourishing as every visit there yields surprise flavors.

They're different, and they're not afraid of being different. Some flavors are better in theory than in practice, but taking those risks in order to be different pays dividends.

Mark Zuckerberg, one of the richest men in the world and the creator of Facebook, insists that risks are imperative in today's business world. "The biggest risk is not taking any risk," Zuckerberg has said. "In a world that is changing really quickly, the only strategy guaranteed to fail is not taking risks."

In 2015 I had the chance to see Johnny Earle, the founder of Johnny Cupcakes, speak at my alma mater during a TEDx event. Johnny Cupcakes is a t-shirt company that hit $4 million in revenue just a few years after opening, and Johnny attributes his company's success to how different they are.

Their t-shirts are nothing extraordinary. In fact, most of them are just a plain t-shirt with a skull and crossbones, but with a cupcake instead of a skull. What makes Johnny Cupcakes is so successful is that they're **very** different from every other t-shirt company. Because of the company name, they're often mistaken for a cupcake shop, and to embrace that confusion their stores look like old-fashioned bakeries, complete with retro ovens, glass displays of their "baked goods" (read: t-shirts), and bakery boxes and bags.

Going to a Johnny Cupcakes store is in itself a different experience, and one that people don't forget. Their t-shirts are also different, and even their sales process is drastically different. One of my favorite examples of a successful t-shirt launch was their "breakfast special" t-shirt. The shirt was breakfast themed – complete with toast, eggs, and bacon in place of a skull and crossbones – and they only sold them for one day before noon (breakfast time!). Because of the different experience and limited availability, the lines at all of their stores were the length of city blocks, so the store served donuts to awaiting customers. Within hours, the t-shirts were sold out in every size. How's that for a different launch!?

At a surface level, it doesn't make sense to only sell a t-shirt before noon. Johnny described one particular customer who walked in at 12:01pm after driving to Boston all the way from New York City in the middle of a snow storm, yet Johnny Cupcakes refused to sell him a shirt. When discussing this in his TEDx presentation, Johnny likened it to buying breakfast at McDonald's and how they do not sell breakfast items once the clock strikes 10:30am. "We wanted to share the same frustrations with our customers," Johnny joked.

Part of Johnny Cupcake's excellence is that they **always** promise a different experience, and that keeps customers coming back.

As promised, this chapter was short, because at the end of the day the important thing to remember is to expect, demand, and commit to *excellence* in every area of your business. A lot of times that means doing something different, and paying attention to *all* of the little things. Every single thing that you do and that you put out into the world represents you and your business, so take care of the little things and you'll see your business flourish.

6

The Biggest Lie in Business: "Competition"

Competition. What is it good for? Absolutely everything!

Perhaps the biggest falsehood that traditional business schools teach is the concept of "competition." As it's taught, competition are your enemies in the marketplace; the alternatives to people buying from your company. In fact, competition is such a scary thing in business school that most professors and business books caution entrepreneurs to not enter markets where there's "too much competition."

In reality, there is rarely such a thing as true "competition." Business is not a zero-sum game, meaning the only way to win isn't if someone else loses. Instead, a rising tide lifts all boats. Most frequently, businesses that should be "competitors" can help each other grow and yield even bigger successes.

I'll give plenty of examples of there not being such a thing as "competition," but first I want to address the elephant in the room: Coca-Cola and Pepsi. When I say that there is no such thing as competition in business, most people point towards big business to show that that may be true on a smaller scale, but on a macro scale they argue that massive corporations do indeed "compete," and that one company's failure is another company's success.

To dispel this large company and large industry myth, look no further than the year 2014. With obesity, diabetes, and other health concerns plaguing the United States, it looked like high-fructose corn syrup sodas were the scapegoat. Governments started passing laws to get sodas out of public schools, and more and more businesses were limiting the sizes of sodas that they served.

Recognizing that competition isn't good for anybody, Pepsi and Coca-Cola teamed up. In 2014 they launched joint marketing efforts to help Americans decrease their sugary drink consumption by one-fifth within a decade. The two major "competitors" jointly agreed to more prominently display their caloric information on their labels, and are reassessing their packaging (in other words, the size of their drinks).

In the face of an industry crisis thanks to health concerns, the two corporate behemoths understood that they'd be better off together.

If you're still not convinced that competition doesn't exist even at a large-scale level, look no further than Apple agreeing to use Google search as its search partner on iPhones around the world. Apple and Google are two of the biggest "competitors" in the world, as they compete on hardware (MacBooks vs. Chrome Books), operating systems (Mac OS vs. Chrome OS), and mobile (iOS vs. Android). Nevertheless, Apple has acknowledged that Google's search engine provides a superior customer experience, and has integrated their search technology into iPhones.

So now that we've dispelled the myth of competition within big business, let's talk about **your** business and **your** competition.

The important thing for you to understand is that *you don't have any competition*. You have **peers** within your market, and if you view them that way then you'll have a huge leg up. When you're starting out, your competition is your best chance at figuring things out quickly, which will save you time and money before you go down the wrong path.

Your "competitors" are great for two things: dissecting their businesses from afar, and probing their businesses from within.

When newpreneurs start their businesses, they have no existing processes, proposals, sales funnels, or automated tools. My favorite role-play to do with newpreneurs is to ask them to sell to me. First of all, it gives them the opportunity to pitch, and then I love seeing what their process is when I say "yes" to becoming their client.

Remember my story from chapter three about my very first paying client with NewGen Consultants? When the local sandwich shop owner said "yes" to becoming a client for our marketing services, we had no idea what was next. We hadn't yet planned for the yes, so we were stumped.

What we could have – and should have! – done is dissect one of our industry peers from within. Most people look at businesses and *wish* they could know how they work on the inside and what their sales "secrets" are. In reality, those secrets are not so secret to people who have gone through the sales process.

So... there's one easy way to figure out what they do to close leads into customers...

...become a lead yourself! When I enter any new market, I always go through a different company's process as a customer. Once the dust settled on our first deal, my business partner and I started studying other internet marketing agencies to see what their offerings were, what their prices were, and what their sales processes looked like. Many times the only way to see what their prices are is to go through the sales process and get pitched to.

I've heard so many pitches from my "competition" that it's crazy. I've been sent their sales brochures, their marketing collateral, and proposals. All of that time I spent as a customer was the best research I could have ever done for my business.

All too often I work with students who stumble the first time they're asked for a proposal. In my opinion, that's inexcusable in today's marketplace. *Every* entrepreneur has the ability to get high-quality proposals from the most successful businesses in their industry by going through the process as a customer.

Are you a photographer who has no clue how to pitch a gig for a bar mitzvah? You're not sure of what price you should charge? You have no clue how the sales process should work? Get off your butt and call a photographer in New York City for an upcoming bar mitzvah and see how they walk you through the process! See what they charge, see how they send you their portfolio, see what their proposal looks like, see what their contract looks like. (Or have a friend do it for you)

This is what I call "dissecting your competitors from within." There's no better way to get a glimpse into the inner workings of your "competition."

If your industry is product-based, you can still go through the entire process by actually buying the product. For example, in 2014 my entire business switched from client-based work to student-based work, meaning rather than working one-on-one with clients I began creating and releasing online programs built for bigger audiences. So rather than having proposals and sales conversations, I had to setup automated systems that would attract students, offer them value, and then sell them into my paid programs.

I always knew that the bigger names in the industry had very refined strategies and tools that maximize profit and give customers customized experiences based on what actions they take, so I decided to start buying products all the time. In fact, most of my closest friends know that still to this day I am constantly buying other people's products and courses just to see how their systems and processes work (and in most cases, I never even end up opening the programs that I paid for!).

One of my earliest discoveries was how the bigger names in the industry use advanced sequencing strategies to speak to their potential customers in a way that resonates more. For example, if I sign up for a free four-part video course, and each video is emailed to me once per day, it doesn't make any sense to email me four days in a row with each video if I never even viewed the first video.

The amateurs in the market will just plaster people's inboxes with these videos, whereas by going through the process as a customer I learned that the high earners in the industry will send you down a different sequence of emails based on your behavior. For example, if a prospect doesn't click the link to view the first video in the free training course, then the next day you can (and should) email them to check in and remind them that they asked for the video, and re-send them the link to the first video.

If they still don't watch the first video, then it doesn't make sense to send the second video, so they go through yet another different series of emails.

This is advanced email marketing that I would have never grasped had I not gone through it myself. It didn't take an expensive course for me to learn this stuff. Instead, my "competition" taught me it for free.

Watch what your competition **does**, not what they **say**. By viewing my competition as a learning opportunity and dissecting their business from within, I learned more than I would have in three years of experimenting on my own. See how valuable your competition is to your success!?

The second technique that I mentioned is dissecting your competitors from the outside. This strategy was particularly useful for me when I had no clue what I was doing with my soccer blog, Premiership Talk. Once I realized that there were bloggers out there making good money, I started studying their websites to figure out what their revenue streams were.

The most obvious revenue stream for websites is advertising revenue. I studied their ad placement (where the ads are on their website), what types of ads they were showing, but most importantly, I started keeping track of which advertisers I saw on their websites.

Once I was confident in my traffic numbers, I started emailing those very same advertisers and asking them if they wanted to advertise on my website. After all, they had already proven that they're open to advertising online, and furthermore they had already proven that they want to advertise on websites just like mine. Boom!

Dissecting a business from the outside can be very fruitful. Success leaves clues, and when you go into the exercise with a keen eye for detail then you'll start to notice all of the little things that make businesses successful.

When I first met my current girlfriend, she was immediately taken aback at my love for shopping malls. I **very rarely** purchase things at shopping malls, but I simply cannot get enough of them. I never turn down the chance to go to the mall. Why? Because I *love* seeing how successful (and not so successful) companies work. I love looking at their branding, where in the store customers go, their signage within the store, and their sales messaging strategies.

To give you an example of the types of things that I notice and think about when I'm at a mall, look no further than my habits when walking by Lindt (the chocolate store with those oh-so-delicious truffles). I love Lindt. What most people don't realize is that Lindt always offers free samples of their truffles… all you need to do is ask.

I've known this fact for a long time, but I rarely take

advantage of it. And trust me, few people love chocolate more than I do!

Why do I never take advantage of it, despite it being free? Because they make it harder to get a free sample than other places. There's a barrier to that free sample... it means I have to walk into the store, talk to an employee, listen to them talk about their different flavors and specials, and then find a way to exit... probably without buying a thing.

That's hard. That's a lot of work. I just want a free truffle!

Contrast that experience to Auntie Anne's, everyone's favorite mall pretzel. Auntie Anne's leaves their free samples right out in the open, with no barriers. You can just walk up and grab a free sample. Their product is great, so they know that they'll convert many of those freebie grabbers into customers.

Even when "all I want is a free sample," because it's so good, I'll often end up in line. No joke... I can never resist Auntie Anne's once a taste of their cinnamon sugar pretzels hits my tongue.

Auntie Anne's would be so much easier to resist if I couldn't so easily get a taste of their product when walking by. The fact that they don't build the same obstacles as Lindt means that I almost always grab myself a free pretzel sample, and I almost always leave the mall with a pretzel in hand. Well, at least pretzel crumbs on my shirt...

You might be thinking that this is a small and insignificant example from a shopping mall, but when I applied this logic to my business it made a huge difference. It's no secret that the way to grow your email marketing list online is to offer something for free in exchange for an email list.

But that's the Lindt approach.

Instead, I've experimented with using the Auntie Anne's approach to email marketing, and rather than building in the barrier of asking someone to give me their email address **before** I ever give them a free sample, I sometimes give them the free content – unguarded, a la Auntie Anne's – and then if they want more of my best stuff, they need to give me their email address. But, if I do my job right and my free content is good enough, then they'll be hooked and want my best stuff. (All it "costs" is an email address!)

This one shopping mall example taught me a valuable lesson: have as few walls in your business as possible, and make it as easy as possible for your potential customers to engage with you.

There are a million other business lessons that I've picked up from walking around shopping malls. Success leaves clues everywhere, and if you tune your eyes and ears into it then you'll start noticing them.

In September 2014 I attended my first ever Camp Good Life Project, and I heard the amazing Jonathan Fields talk about *patterns*. I've always been an observant person, but when I listened to Jonathan – one of the most successful and inspiring entrepreneurs I've ever met, and definitely the most brilliant that I've met! – talk about how he recognizes patterns everywhere in life, my observations became more intentional and more effective.

Recognizing patterns is one step beyond being observant. Not only does Jonathan notice things, but he remembers what struck him. When he looks at businesses, he keeps track of what he liked, what he didn't like, and what he'd improve on. Over time, patterns emerge, and those guide his actions.

When I started implementing this within my own life and business, it made instant improvements. I've always loved watching great speakers speak, and I was always cognizant of *why* I thought they were a great speaker, but I never sat down and tried to identify patterns among these great speakers.

Since hearing Jonathan speak about patterns, though, I started making a list. Any time I saw a speaker that I thought was great, I'd jot down notes about them. After seeing a few great speakers, the patterns were crystal clear. These patterns revolved around not only their content and delivery, but also around their clothes, their introductions, and their posture during speeches.

Look at your competitors with the intention of identifying patterns in what makes them successful.

One activity that I love to do while dissecting businesses from the outside is to identify their profit-helping and profit-hurting aspects. For example, if a business has a fantastic sales page, that's a profit-helping attribute. If a business has a confusing listing of their products and packages, that's profit-hurting.

For each of these product-helping and product-hurting attributes, I ask myself one question: how can I make this better?

If you look at your competitors and you can make even their best and most profit-helping attributes even better, then you'll have a bright future. If I was starting a burger joint, I'd go to Five Guys and ask how I can make everything better from a customer perspective. For example, one of Five Guys' best experiences as a customer is their fountain soda machine. It has just about every flavor of soda you can think of, and the machine itself is pretty cool! But... I'd still ask myself "how can I make this even better?"

Finally, when it comes to your "competition," remember that behind those businesses are real, live people, just like you and I. The single smartest thing I did when I was 19 years old and just started Premiership Talk was I emailed all of my "competitors" to introduce myself. (Remember when I said to be naïve? Here's another great example)

By emailing them all personally, most of them responded with welcoming words, and offered to hop on a Skype call with me. During those Skype calls I learned *a ton*, and those put me so far ahead of the curve that my growth was rapidly accelerated.

Not-so-coincidentally, all of the "competitors" that never replied to my email were the ones that weren't around a year later. Successful people and successful businesses are always willing to help, because they know that growth in the industry across the board can help their own businesses grow.

Working with my "competition" was such a cornerstone to my success within my first few years that my first thought was always "how can I incorporate my other fellow soccer website owners?"

When you first start a blog, the most difficult thing in the world is to get traffic. You can post like crazy on Facebook, Twitter, StumbleUpon, and other websites, and that will get you an initial bump in website traffic, but it's not sustainable at the beginning.

Instead, I had the idea of "guest posting" on my competitors' websites. I offered to write content (for free) specifically made for their website, in exchange for a link back to my own website. This worked wonders... I was able to leverage their larger, more established audiences, and if my content was good (like Auntie Anne's pretzels!), then they'd click through to my website and become part of my audience. The competitors who let me do this were smart because they had an abundance mindset; they knew that web traffic was abundant, and by sharing it with me it wouldn't hurt their own business. (The opposite, of course, is a scarcity mindset, where most website owners wouldn't want to share their traffic with me because they'd view it as me "stealing" or "taking" their visitors)

The websites who allowed me to guest post also "won" because they got additional traffic. I always promoted my posts on their website, which got them more traffic. Win-wins do exist in business and in life!

When my site's traffic plateaued, I again thought about how I could incorporate my so-called competition. I realized that there were probably a bunch of other website owners who were having the same problem, so I figured that if we banded together then we could all help each other.

In 2009, the Premiership Talk Banner Exchange was born. In the banner exchange, 20 member sites all placed a snippet of code (supplied by me) onto their websites, and the code displayed a different member website's banner advertisement, with a link to their site. This way we all shared our audiences together, and advertised for each other. Together, all of our audiences grew.

As we got bigger, we implemented a token system into the banner exchange so that we could welcome smaller websites into the exchange. The more a website displayed other websites' banners, they earned more tokens, which meant that their banner was displayed on more websites. Smaller websites that we welcomed maybe only had 100 visitors per day, so they earned 100 tokens, which meant that their banner was displayed 100 times on other, bigger websites. By instituting this, we could welcome sites of all sizes, which helped them grow even more.

As the banner exchange became more and more successful and all of our websites started growing, we took these informal working relationships even further by sharing advertising deals. Major advertisers would approach one of the bigger sites in the network, and we'd turn those deals into even larger advertising deals by offering ad space on a network of websites rather than just one.

I tell you these stories not because I think that they will directly impact your business. Chances are your business will be drastically different from Premiership Talk, and more than likely you won't have the chance to create a banner exchange with your competitors. But, I tell you these stories to illustrate the power of working *with* your "competitors," and turning your competitors into your peers.

Before we finish dissecting your competitors, I want to introduce you to some tech tools that you can use to further lift the lid on their businesses. First, SimilarWeb.com can show you a **ton** of invaluable data about their website and their traffic sources. And it's free!

In the spirit of my shopping mall examples from earlier, let's pretend that you're looking to start a pretzel bakery. If you plug AuntieAnnes.com into SimilarWeb, it reveals their traffic sources, paid advertising strategies, and information about their audience. The raw numbers that SimilarWeb displays are usually very off-base (for example, SimilarWeb estimates that their website gets 40,000 visitors per month, but in fact I'm willing to wager that they get more than that).

But, using the tool, I have learned that 12% of their traffic is direct, whereas the remainder is referral traffic (20%, which comes from other websites on the internet linking to them) and search traffic (68%, which comes from organic search engine searches and paid search engine advertising campaigns).

By further looking into the SimilarWeb report, I can see that most people who find AuntieAnnes.com organically through search engine searches are searching for words like "pretzel" and "Auntie Anne's" (duh).

But... here's the most interesting finding. Thanks to SimilarWeb, I found a revenue stream that I would have never thought of for Auntie Anne's. Their biggest paid advertising campaign on Google is for the keyword "fundraising ideas." I dug a little deeper into that, and it turns out that Auntie Anne's offers to team up with schools, companies, and non-profits to sell goods to raise money. If you're interested in seeing that strategy in action, their dedicated fundraising page is located at auntieannes.com/more/fundraising

That's a revenue stream that I would have never thought of if I was starting a pretzel baking business, but now I know that I could approach local schools, sports leagues, and other non-profits to help them with fundraising through selling my delicious pretzels! Brilliant! Thanks for that idea, Auntie Anne's!

SimilarWeb also shows me which social networks Auntie Anne's focuses on. 49% of their social media traffic is from Facebook, with 32% coming from Twitter. The rest of their social media traffic is driven by YouTube, Reddit, and Yahoo! Answers, which isn't something that I would have expected, but opens up new opportunities for me as a new pretzel baker.

The second (free) tool that you can use to dissect your competitors' businesses is Facebook Audience Insights. Sticking to the example of Auntie Anne's, I see that they currently have just shy of 1 million people who like them on Facebook. Using Facebook Audience Insights I can dig deeper into understanding *who* these people are that are so loyal to Auntie Anne's that they like them on Facebook.

If you've never used Audience Insights before, you can just Google it and you'll get the direct link to it. Once I plug "Auntie Anne's" in to the Interests section, it shows me information on their 1 million followers.

Based on Facebook's data, I now know that a staggering 80% of their Facebook likes are female. Incredibly,

53% of those females are between the ages of 18 and 24, so clearly Auntie Anne's dominates the younger age groups.

You may be thinking "but Brian, ages 18 to 24 are popular on Facebook, so of course that's the make-up of their likes." The Audience Insights tool shows you what the population of Facebook's user base is so that you can compare it and see if they are over-indexing in that age group. In this case, only 19.2% of Facebook's females are between the ages of 18 and 24, so Auntie Anne's audience is hugely over-indexing within this age group, suggesting that it's a core part of their customer composition. As you move up in ages, Auntie Anne's appeal lessens exponentially. For example, only 2% of their female audience is aged 65+, whereas 9.5% of Facebook's overall female users fall into this category.

So as an entrepreneur, I can use this information to my advantage when it comes to my marketing. I should be using language and imagery that appeals to the younger female audience, because they've already proven that they *love* Auntie Anne's.

Besides just basic demographic information, Facebook, with its treasure-trove of data, gives lifestyle information about audiences. Auntie Anne's most popular lifestyle category is "Apple Pie Families." Facebook's description of an "Apple Pie Family" is "upper-middle class couples with school-age children. They are homeowners, often minivan drivers, and avid radio listeners."

If you're a pretzel baker, you just gained valuable insight into who responds to your market.

On top of all of that data, Facebook keeps going. Facebook can show you which other pages on Facebook Auntie Anne's audience likes so that you can know their other interests, it shows you the locations of their audience, how engaged their audience is (for example, do they click a lot of ads on Facebook? Do they like a lot of posts on Facebook? Do they share a lot of posts on Facebook?), and information about their household income and purchase behavior.

Remember – Facebook has mountains of data on each and every one of us Facebook users (there's over 1.5 **billion** active users on Facebook every month!), so they can tell us entrepreneurs a lot of valuable information about our competitors… and ourselves.

Networking with Your Competitors

Before we close this chapter, I want to discuss networking with competitors. Clearly I think it's a fantastic strategy to get to know your competitors, but all too often I see newpreneurs trying and failing to establish an ongoing relationship with their competitors.

If you're starting a service-based business, you should approach your competitors in two ways. First, it's encouraged to reach out and have an initial conversation to introduce yourself and ask as many questions as possible. That's precisely what I did with the major bloggers in my industry when I started Premiership Talk.

But after that, don't make the mistake of constantly wanting to meet with them or Skype with them… that's not how you establish an ongoing working relationship. Instead, only reach out with one of three things: 1) to help them or provide some value, even if it's as small as sharing a helpful article that they may benefit from, 2) if you have an idea for an opportunity for the two of you to work together, or 3) if it's been a while and you just want to say hello, provide a short update on what you've been up to, and to ask if you can help with anything.

The common problem with most emails from newpreneurs is that they build up barriers and obstacles to people responding to their emails by making it difficult and time-intensive to respond. Whenever I speak at a school or nonprofit event, I always have students and people email me afterwards with a bunch of questions. I'm always happy to help, but if they make it difficult by emailing back a few months later and saying "what are you up to?" then I have to sit down and formulate a response about what I'm up to... and typically I have a lot going on!

But, by emailing me and just saying "Hey! It's been a while. Here's what I'm up to. Are you working on anything I can help with?" then you make it easier for me to respond. I get to digest what you're doing and will likely ask a follow-up question to engage you if I have the time, and you haven't put the onus on me to come up with a well-written and thought-out response giving an overview of "what I'm up to." Make it easy for people to respond to you.

When I was running NewGen Consultants, many fellow marketing agencies networked with us and wanted to team up with us on projects. But, they made it difficult to do that. They weren't comfortable setting firm agreements in place, so we never knew when we could turn to them or not. Because of that, we often turned to the internet when we needed graphic designers, because it was so easy to work with them... there were no barriers.

The most successful experience I've had with this was with a local web designer in Boston. She created websites for businesses all across the United States, and we teamed up with her to offer our Search Engine Optimization services on her clients' websites. We made our prices clear so she could communicate them clearly with her potential clients (and existing clients), and always knew exactly what we could and would do.

By doing this, she was able to offer a whole new service line, and it made her stand out in a crowded scene of web designers.

The keys to this successful agreement were:

1. We made our prices completely transparent and known to her, so it was easy for her to work with us.

2. We gave her **all** of our marketing collateral and resources, so she would better understand exactly what we do and so she could communicate it to her clients.

3. We were extremely accessible for her via phone and email, so she knew she could count on us.

Rather than wasting her time and ours by always wanting to "network" with her and go on coffee dates, we made it easy to work with us and do business with us. Our first meeting was to get to know each other and plant the seed for working together in the future, and our second meeting was when we laid out what it looks like to work with each other on projects.

The next communication we had? She had a client for us, who turned into one of our longest paying monthly clients. That's effective networking. We made it easy for her to say "yes" to our arrangement since we had the majority of the logistics figured out, and gave her everything she'd need to refer clients to us.

When you're starting your business, your best resources are in fact your competitors. Dissect their businesses from the outside and the inside. Go through their sales process as a customer, talk to them, use the tools I've outlined for you here, and see patterns when you're observing the world. And, never forget to **work with your competition.**

7

Your Biggest Threat: Haters

Ah, we've reached my favorite topic of entrepreneurship: haters. I personally lump doubters and skeptics into the category of haters, so in this chapter we're going to discuss all three.

If you're not familiar with the term hater, I'll defer to the *Urban Dictionary* definition:

Hater (n): A person that simply cannot be happy for another person's success. So rather than be happy they make a point of exposing a flaw in that person. Hating, the result of being a hater, is not exactly jealousy. The hater doesn't really want to be the person he or she hates, rather the hater wants to know someone else down a notch.

Urban Dictionary's example of a hater gets even better:

Susan: You know, Kevin from accounting is doing very well. He just bought a house in a very nice part of town.

Jane (hater): If he is doing so well why does he drive that '89 Taurus?

Look – depending on where you are in your entrepreneurial journey, you may or may not realize it, but when you try to do *anything*, there will be haters.

One of my favorite quotes of all time is "There is only one way to avoid criticism: Do nothing, say nothing, be nothing."

Our society is setup with a certain set of expectations: go to college, get a job, work for 40+ years, and retire. Entrepreneurs like you and I question and avoid that typical path, which raises eyebrows and makes people uncomfortable with their own choices in life.

Which leads me to my first major point: when you encounter haters (and you will), they're actually not hating on you because of **you**... they're hating on you because you're making them question **themselves** and their own life choices.

Early on in my journey with Premiership Talk, I encountered haters in the form of comment trolls. People from around the world would leave comments criticizing me for writing blog posts or criticize the website, or even just writing negative things such as "Who is Brian Lofrumento and who gave him a keyboard?"

At first it bothered me. But then I realized that those people had nothing against me personally, and really didn't hate my work. After all, they were continually logging on to my website. (By the way, thanks for the advertising views!)

What I realized is that they were upset with themselves for just being average and never having the guts or determination to put their own views out into the world. They were hiding behind their keyboards and anonymously writing hate comments so that they could feel better about themselves. After all, nothing that they said was productive or constructive, so there was no value to it other than blowing off steam for themselves.

As Premiership Talk grew, I saw more and more different types of haters. I don't want this to seem like it was a difficult journey and everyone was against me. On the contrary, throughout my entire entrepreneurial life I've felt like I've had nothing but support from all angles, but life has a funny way of making a little bit of hate or doubt cloud out the many supporters.

Throughout that, I realized that there are three stages of haters for *all* entrepreneurs. The more I met other entrepreneurs, the more I learned that we all experience these three stages. I'm outlining these for you here while you're transitioning from a wantrepreneur to an entrepreneur so that you can identify these people, understand them, and be fueled by them rather than taking it personally. So here are the three stages of haters:

The Status Quo Haters

Status quo haters hate people who are doing something that questions the status quo. Status quo haters love, well, the status quo. These haters appear long before you enjoy any success, which means they're your biggest threat when you're just starting out, because they try to discourage you enough that you never even leave the status quo.

Once a status quo hater hears that you're trying to do something extraordinary, they'll immediately start hating. Sometimes they'll say "man, that's a stupid idea" to second-guess yourself.

Other times they'll be more explicit and outright try to dishearten you. Don't be surprised to hear a status-quo hater say something like "that will never work" or "too many other people are doing that already."

Status quo haters will hate on anyone who is doing something outside of the status quo. Why? Because they love the status quo. If you're trying to do something to elevate yourself, these haters will immediately pounce because you're making them uncomfortable and you're suggesting that there's something better.

Status quo haters probably choose mediocrity. Sometimes this means they're a bum that doesn't do anything, but don't be fooled... many times this type of hater can have a good job and an okay life. But they think that's as good as it gets. They're convinced the path that they're following is the righteous one, and your decision to do something extraordinary is threatening that vision.

The ultimate threat to a status quo hater is **you. You** are making them question if their path is best. This makes them uncomfortable, so they'll hate and try to drag you back into the status quo.

The Milestone Haters

Once you actually get started and build some momentum up you'll almost immediately enjoy your first milestone. This can mean a lot of things: your first customer, your first big deal, your first big break, your first publicity, etc. It's your first marker of success and what's to come.

...but nothing brings out the haters like your first big milestone of success. Milestone haters are quick to hate, but chances are they won't do it publicly. After all, it's hard to hate after you've just accomplished some level of success.

Instead, milestone haters will privately hate on you to their friends and anyone else who will listen. If you used to hang out with them, they'll probably start distancing themselves, and they won't share in your successes at all. Why? Don't worry, it's nothing personal. It's not that they hate you or are jealous of **you**, they're actually mad at **themselves.**

Your success has seriously thrown all of their life decisions into focus. They're wondering if **they** should have rejected the status quo and tried something extraordinary. They're wondering if **they'll** ever experience something like the milestone that you've just reached. They're wondering if **they** are heading down the right path. You've done this to them... you've shown what's possible, and as a result you've made them question their own life decisions. You little devil, you.

These haters are really only dangerous in one way: they can slow your momentum down. Countless studies have shown that our happiness in life isn't determined by how many trusted people we can turn to when we have bad times, but our happiness is more greatly impacted when we have trusted people to turn to in **good times**. Don't let the milestone hater kill your momentum and your happiness when they're not celebrating your successes with you.

When you reach your milestone, the milestone hater will probably try to knock you down a step by saying something along the lines of "yeah, but how much money did you make from that publicity?" Or "yeah, but how much have you made overall?" Don't let them knock you down and ruin your momentum. Understand why they're hating - it's about **them**, not **you** (remember, you're threatening) - and just turn to your true supporters to share in your success and excitement.

The Too-Late Haters

These haters are the most abundant and most vocal. While status quo haters will hate just to you, the too-late haters will be far more public with their hate. These are the haters that leave blog comments, talk about you in large social circles, and think about you while you're enjoying your successes.

Too-late haters appear once you've truly enjoyed success. You've had quite a few milestones, and it's clear that you're a force to be reckoned with. Unlike the two types of haters previously, these haters are past the point of you threatening them. You no longer threaten them by forcing them to question their own decisions... now they're just jealous. They realize that your success is so great that it's too late for them to do anything about it.

Don't let their jealousy impact you. In fact, you shouldn't even see it, nevermind think about it or respond to it. Delete their blog comments, YouTube comments, and social media comments. Use it as fuel to drive on. Always remind yourself to be polite and helpful to **everyone** you encounter in life. Don't react and drop down to their level. Because here's the secret... there's only one way a too-late hater can beat you: by making you step down to their level, even if it's only for one second. Don't give them that satisfaction.

Unexpected Haters

Besides the three stages of haters that I outlined on the previous pages, as you begin your entrepreneurial journey you'll encounter unexpected haters. When I was a new entrepreneur, it was these haters that affected me the most, because I was confused and surprised at the feelings that I got from them.

The most unexpected of all is what I call **well-wishing haters**. These people are ones that want the best for you, but say things that unintentionally knock you down and make you question your own path. Because these people mean so much to you, their words make you want to stop what you're doing and take the easy road.

The greatest example of well-wishing haters is your own family. If you're going out on your own and starting a business, no one cares more about you than your family, so they're worried for you. They want to see the best for you, so they worry about what will happen if things don't work. Remember – society was trained to believe that entrepreneurship is risky, and somehow they've been fooled to think that working for someone else who can fire them in a second is less risky.

As such, they say things like "well why don't you go to school in case things don't work out." Or "just work part-time so you have some money." Or "you have to think about the long-run." These are all statements that family members and close friends might say to you as you embark on the most exciting journey of your life, and they're all statements said out of fear. Fear for the unknown.

Indeed, these well-wishing haters don't mean to hate. In fact, they would be **shocked** to know that you view their comments as hating. And that's why they hurt most of all... because you know that they're said out of a position of love and caring.

These people are *worriers*, and they don't understand that they are trying to transfer their fear to us entrepreneurs. They don't understand that their pleas for us to play it safe and accept the status quo knock us back when we've got more important things to figure out and focus on.

These well-wishing haters believe that they're being caring and protective. But what you need to know as a newpreneur is that they mean well, and you must learn to separate their fear from reality and from your future. They only know one path (the status quo), and they believe it's the best for you. Look at it as an opportunity to show them what's possible.

Perhaps the most challenging thing about dealing with well-wishing haters is that because they're so close to us, they are constantly around us and constantly in our ears. And because they're so close to us, their words carry more weight. It's the loving uncle that says "oh, are you *still* doing that?"

Identify it. And move past it.

When the voices are so constant and close to you, you'll need to build iron-clad walls to block out the doubt. The most dangerous thing in the world for a new entrepreneur is that they let doubting voices creep into their mind. As an entrepreneur, you need to be steel-hearted, determined, and confident in what lays ahead. Nothing great was accomplished by playing it safe.

Talking about doubt and your mind leads me into the next category of unexpected haters: **yourself.** It sounds counter-intuitive, but the biggest hater that you'll come across throughout your entrepreneurial journey is your own mind.

At the end of the day, no one talks to you as much as you talk to yourself, and it's inevitable that self-doubt will creep into your mind. The biggest thing that I've seen trigger self-doubt in entrepreneurs' minds is comparing themselves to others.

There are two types of peoples that we entrepreneurs often compare ourselves to: other entrepreneurs, and corporate employees.

The danger of comparing ourselves to other entrepreneurs who we see enjoying success is that too often we compare our chapter 1 to their chapter 20. Especially as a newpreneur, you need to be careful when comparing yourself to someone else, as you don't know the challenges and failures that they've **already gone through** to get where they are.

On the flip side, it's so easy to look at your old college friends, your friends from home, or people that you know from other walks of life who are in corporate jobs and question your own path. Especially when you see someone else get a promotion or get a raise, it's easy to feel down on yourself.

The important thing to remember is that you're on an entirely different path that isn't comparable to theirs. Chances are they will look at your life and be envious of the fact that you work for yourself, that you have a flexible schedule, and that you don't rely on 2% raises each year. In fact, you, unlike them, have the ability to make as much money as you want this year... without having someone else tell you what to do, and without spending 40+ hours in an office each week, with limited vacation time.

Things that other people say have a way of sticking in our heads, so the best way to overcome the negative words that other people say to you is to just **stop caring what other people think**. It sounds harsh, but if you care about other people's opinions about you then you'll fall back into the endless and unrewarding loop of having your most important life decisions decided by society's expectations.

Another one of my favorite quotes is "a tiger doesn't lose sleep over the opinion of sheep." Be dogged in your pursuit of success, and just fly past any and all doubters that try to put discouraging remarks in your head. Even when it's family telling you things to try to "look out for you," stop caring what they think and know that you'll prove them wrong through hard work, commitment, and determination.

Another way to overcome self-doubt and get outside of your own head is to use the 30-60-90 method of goals. From the productivity chapter you already know that I like focusing on bite-sized activities, and the same holds true for goals. When setting goals, I always have a 30-day goal, a 60-day goal, and a 90-day goal.

Doing this accomplishes two things. First of all, in the face of possible self-doubt (and doubt from others), there are three very clear goals in mind, each of which are just on the horizon. This is great because if we're chasing a goal that's years down the line then it will be harder to overcome self-doubt. When the goals are so far away, our self-doubt can become even greater because there's more uncertainty about what will happen a year from now, two years from now, or five years from now. Set goals that are just around the corner and you'll feel like you have more control to actually get there, erasing much of the uncertainty.

The second thing the 30-60-90 goal method accomplishes is that it keeps your mind so busy chasing after these three goals that you stay on track and don't even have time for that self-doubt talk inside your own head.

Even with these techniques, though, self-doubt will still creep into your mind at times. I'm no psychologist, so I can't explain the inner workings of the human brain, but I can suggest one activity that I've found completely changes my thoughts: express gratitude. When you're having a rough day and are starting to question your own path, your own credentials, your own knowledge, and your own worth in the market, take a few minutes to sit down with just yourself and consider all of the things that you're grateful for.

I personally like to come up with ten things that I'm grateful for whenever I need a positive boost, and after doing this exercise for so many years it's become easy to do that. It not only puts me in a great mood, but it erases any self-doubt that may have been lingering.

Who Are You Surrounded By?

The most important consideration for all entrepreneurs when it comes to nullifying haters and self-doubt is to surround yourself with remarkable people who lift you up. It's no secret that you are the average of the five people who you spend the most time with, so choose your five people carefully.

Look around at the five people who you spend the most time with, and you can figure out how much money you'll make, what your attitude towards life will be like, how much you'll weigh (it's true – research studies have shown that hanging out with overweight people will make you overweight), and how hard you work. You are the average of the five people who you spend the most time with.

One of the biggest shifts in my entrepreneurial life has been to erase the haters, talkers (all talk but no action), and quitters from my life. Peter Voogd, an accomplished author and successful entrepreneur, revealed in his book *The Entrepreneur's Blueprint to Massive Success*, that Grant Cardone (a multi-millionaire entrepreneur) once told him that "if you still have all the same friends you had in high school you probably haven't grown very much."

It sounds harsh, and it doesn't have to be so definitive, but the message is that if you remain friends with someone simply because you grew up with them and despite their lack of a positive influence on your life, then you need to re-assess your choice of friends. These haters, talkers, and quitters all can have a negative impact on your energy and determination to succeed, and it's okay to let them go as you grow. Or, even when you just *decide* that you're going to grow. There's no time better than the present.

Surround yourself with people who bring you up. Surround yourself with people who value doing something that has an impact rather than wasting their days playing video games or being miserable. It's okay to have fun, and by all means I don't think anyone can expect to be surrounded by all entrepreneurs or people who are changing the world, but be cognizant of the effect that the people around you have on your life.

Stop Hanging Out with Lobsters

In 2015 I attended my first ever World Domination Summit, an event hosted every year in Portland, Oregon. The event was the biggest collection of brilliant minds that I've ever seen, as 3,500 entrepreneurs and world-changers all converged on Portland for an incredible three days of inspiring speakers, deep connections, and adventure.

One of the speakers that had the most profound impact on the audience was Jon Acuff. Jon is a New York Times bestselling author, and has spoken in front of hundreds of thousands of people and major companies all across the world. As an accomplished entrepreneur, Jon knows what it takes to go past all of the negative talk, haters, and self-doubt.

As a fellow Massachusetts native, Jon spent a lot of time on the ocean, especially considering he grew up on the north shore. In his presentation at World Domination Summit, Jon told the story of observing birds building beautiful nests inside old, broken down lobster cages.

The birds were brilliant to use these old artifacts as lots for their homes as they wouldn't be disrupted by humans, and they had a frame to build their nests around.

As Jon pointed out, though, if the birds were to ask lobsters if it was a good idea to build their nests there, the lobsters would immediately reply that the cages are death, and they should stay as far away from them as possible.

Jon's point with the story and his observations is that often we get "bird ideas and then ask all the lobsters in our life to approve them." Of course, the lobsters in our life will describe these bird ideas as horrible and risky, despite the fact that the lobster cages were a *perfect* setting for birds to flourish in.

The reason why Jon's presentation resonated with so many people in the audience is because he went on to suggest that not only are we all surrounded by lobsters in many cases, but that we often *actively seek out lobsters* because we **want** them to disagree with what we're doing so that we don't have to do it.

Think about that for a second. All too often we look for people to disagree with what we're doing so we don't have to do it.

According to Jon, "if our internal voices are saying 'you suck,' 'someone has already done this,' and you can find one other person to agree, then we have consensus, and then you don't have to do it. Sometimes we'll find haters because they'll confirm the things we think are secretly true."

Jon's point with his presentation was to **quit hanging out with lobsters.** Quit hanging out with people that fill your mind with doubts and that tell you that it's a bad idea to do something different.

In his book *The Magic of Thinking Big*, Dr. David J. Schwartz reveals a way to identify people who have a small and limited mind and a negative mindset. He says that if you tell someone who accepts mediocrity that you're going to own a large and expensive home – like, say, a mansion in Beverly Hills – then they'll laugh at you. If you say the exact same thing to someone who already owns an expensive mansion, though, then they won't laugh at you. **Because they know it's possible.**

This concept is true for mankind at all levels, even in high school. Remember the kids who made fun of the kids who were getting good grades? They were trying to hold the smarter kid back because they were self-conscious and disappointed in their *own* grades. Chances are today they're still too busy knocking others rather than lifting themselves up and improving their situation. You don't need good grades to be successful, but you can't be negative and small-minded if you want to be successful.

You can easily identify the people in your life who have small and limited minds by their reactions to your grand ideas. "Big men do not laugh at big ideas," Dr. Schwartz wrote in his book. "People who tell you it cannot be done almost always are unsuccessful people, are strictly average, or mediocre at best, when it comes to accomplishment." As he says, "the opinion of these people can be poison."

Dr. Schwartz gives the best defense against negativity, by saying that you should only accept negative advice as a challenge to prove that you *can* do it.

So why in a book about going from wantrepreneur to entrepreneur did I include an entire chapter on haters, even though they'll do nothing positive for your journey from wantrepreneur to entrepreneur? Because the reality is that you'll face them, and they'll be your biggest threat to success.

The reality is that you need to be able to identify haters and separate their lobster thoughts from reality, and push through your own self-doubt so that you can relentlessly pursue your dreams. Coming across haters is inevitable, so if you're armed with this knowledge and understanding of *why* they hate (because you're making them question themselves and their own path), and *how* to overcome them then you'll nullify their threat.

8

Entrepreneurship 101: Business Isn't Rocket Science

You may be wondering why a book about how to become an entrepreneur has so little step-by-step business action items. First of all, the pages before this one contain all of the most important things for newpreneurs. Second of all, mixed in with all of the anecdotes and tips that I've written about are some of the best business lessons you'll need as you start your first company. Third of all, you could be starting *any* company in the world – from a web design agency to a company that herds cattle for older farmers (what?) – so it's nearly impossible to cover actionable steps that you'll need to take without knowing your exact business.

But fourth of all – and above all else – is because **business isn't rocket science**. In fact, launching a successful business boils down to three steps:

1) Deciding who you serve

2) Creating a solution to their problems

3) Figuring out *where* your potential customers are, and getting in front of them there so they can buy your solution

Deciding who you serve is a step that most entrepreneurs skip. I've been guilty of the same, as has every entrepreneur that I've ever met. All too often we work to bring solutions to the marketplace, and then we try to find customers for that solution. Instead, the most successful businesses **find products for their customers**.

This is a helpful point for you even if you don't have a

business idea. By deciding who you want to serve, dozens of business ideas will become immediately apparent. Some examples of who you might want to serve are accountants, people looking to buy their first home, restaurant owners, amateur bowlers, bloggers, or people who just bought their first Mac. You can literally choose **anyone** who you want to serve, because any group of people that you choose will have their own set of problems, and you can build solutions to those problems.

One of my favorite real life examples of serving an audience is Pat Flynn, the owner of the *Smart Passive Income* blog. Pat regularly makes over $100,000 **per month** from his blog, but when he started his business in 2008 he made $0 per month... just like you.

Pat's first business was born out of his desire to pass the LEED exam (Leadership in Energy and Environmental Design, a popular accreditation among architects). As someone who wanted to pass the test himself, Pat identified a problem within that market: the study materials were overwhelming and cumbersome. As a result, Pat started a simple WordPress website for himself and for others in the same boat as him, specifically coworkers and fellow test-studiers on LEED forums. Pat knew that he wanted to serve people taking the LEED exam, and he knew what the problem was.

From there, Pat just started providing free value to the people he wanted to serve. He started publishing his study notes on his website, and freely shared the links to his study material on industry forums and with coworkers. In other words, he began solving the problem faced by the people he wanted to serve. Yes, even if you start something because you're primarily solving one of your own problems, there are likely thousands – if not millions – of people just like you facing that same problem. By choosing to serve yourself, you're also choosing to serve them, so don't discount that as a way to identify and start your first business.

In 2008 Pat decided that he wanted to more formally serve the market as his main business after getting laid off from his corporate job, so by the time it came to making a product, he already knew exactly how to best serve his market: give them a streamlined way to study for and pass the LEED exam. Thus, GreenExamAcademy.com was born, and Pat made nearly $8,000 in October of 2008, shortly after getting laid off from his job.

Pat's story is inspiring and insightful because it shows how he first tackled the decision of identifying **who** he wanted to serve. It started with serving himself, but at the same time he acknowledged that his coworkers and fellow young professionals in the architecture industry all were in similar situations. Then, he identified the **problem** that those people were facing: no good way to pass the LEED exam, which typically took *years* to pass.

Finally, Pat was able to create a product (his notes) that best served the market. Already having identified the people he wanted to serve and their main problem that he wanted to solve, Pat created his first product: a $199 ebook containing his notes and strategies to pass the test. Hundreds of sales later, Pat had made more in his first month of selling that ebook than he did in his corporate job. That's how you start a business!

Picking who you want to serve and a problem that you want to solve is easy, but most people get tripped up on how to actually find **buyers** within that market who are willing to pay money for the solution.

This is the quintessential marketing conundrum. Given a product, how do you find buyers?

Regardless of your industry, your product, your service, or your business, the answer is **always the same**. To find customers, you need to identify **where** your potential customers are, and go there. In Pat's case, his potential customers were people studying for the LEED exam, and he knew that they hung out on certain forums where young architect professionals discussed the exam. If you're a real estate agent who targets first-time home buyers, it might not be so easy to figure out where your potential customers are, because they don't necessarily congregate in a physical place. Using the internet, though, you know that they all "hang out" on Google's search pages for search terms like "first time home buyer tax breaks" or "how to buy your first home." In that case, your marketing should focus on getting you onto those search result pages, so that people searching those terms will find you.

For NewGen Consultants, my marketing agency that I launched in 2012, our ideal customers were solopreneurs (entrepreneurs running their business by themselves) who needed more customers and clients. We knew exactly where these solopreneurs hung out... they were at BNI (Business Network International) meetings and Chamber of Commerce events. Why were these such effective places to be marketing? Because consider the motives of a small business owner who goes to BNI or Chamber of Commerce events. There's really only two reasons that they might be going: 1) they're looking to network with other professionals so they can maybe collaborate together, or 2) they're looking to network with other professionals so they can generate referrals and get new customers. In the latter case, we knew that they were looking for a new way to get customers, and our solution (internet marketing) could help them accomplish that.

For Premiership Talk, I knew who my ideal customers were: companies who sold products related to soccer, who wanted to target soccer fans. (Remember, your **customers** are the people who pay you! My readers were my audience, but not my customers). I knew exactly where these companies were... they were advertising on other websites, so I went there to get their contact information and then reached out to them via phone, Skype, and email.

Lead with Value

Over the years, I've gotten better at business. I've been able to grow businesses quicker and make more revenue, and it's thanks to one major shift in my business philosophy. Since the tail end of 2013, my entire business strategy has been to **lead with value**.

No matter what your business is, you have the opportunity to **lead with value**, which will make your entire business grow quicker and will streamline your lead generation efforts.

Leading with value means that your first interaction with people should always revolve around you **giving value**. Too many businesses start their interactions with potential customers by pitching their products and services, long before they've ever proven their value.

One way that my marketing agency grew rapidly was when we consciously decided to lead with value. We did this in quite a few different ways. First, we began hosting in-person seminars and workshops for local small business owners, where we taught them how to use their websites to generate more customers and clients. We gave free admission to these seminars and workshops, offering free food and an hour of us giving away some of our best content and information.

One of my favorite moments in business came at the end of our very first free seminar that we offered. At the end of my presentation, I asked the audience of 15 small business owners if they had any questions, and one of them raised his hand and said "Yeah... where do I cut the check!?" Boom – just one hour of giving away free content and leading with value convinced this small business owner to work with us.

By leading with value in this manner, we no longer needed to *convince* businesses to work with us. By giving away value, **they convinced themselves** that they wanted to work with us. When you show people how valuable you are and you are more than willing to help them, that makes selling them a million times easier than if you approach them in a "salesy" way.

Before we knew any better, we used to attend networking events, tell people what we did, and tried to get them to listen to us on a "strategy session" call, which was nothing more than us talking about what we could do for them and then giving our sales pitch. We enjoyed limited success when pitching people, but even if you're the best salesman in the world, it can't compare to leading with value.

It's always disappointing to hear newpreneurs talk about how they struggle to close prospects into sales. So often I hear them say the word "convince." The old way of doing business involves a lot of convincing... first you need to convince people that they should let you tell them about what you do, then you need to convince people that they need what you do, then you need to convince people that they need **you** to do what you do, and finally you need to convince people they need to **pay you** to do what you do. Excuse my abruptness, but that sucks. "Convincing people" isn't fun, and it doesn't feel good.

Instead, lead with value. Stop caring about convincing people to work with you, and just give away as much value as possible. They'll then convince themselves.

When my business partner and I started NewGen Consultants, we knew we didn't want to cold call people. Still, we tried. We tried cold-emailing businesses across the country to get them to jump on a phone call with us and hear us talk about why they needed Search Engine Optimization.

It didn't work. We weren't leading with value, even though our emails made it crystal clear that the reason why we believed they needed SEO was so that they could get more business and make more money.

Soon after we changed our strategy, and we started sending out in-depth SEO analyses to business owners. We paid for a software tool that could analyze a website and give recommendations for actionable step-by-step improvements for a website, and we started sending those customized reports individually to businesses that we wanted to work with. Rather than trying to sell them, we gave them incredible value (these reports cost us hundreds of dollars per month to generate), and we didn't try to sell them. Once they read through the recommendations and saw the results that they'd get by implementing those recommendations, they had already convinced themselves that they wanted to work with us.

To take it a step further, whenever we sent proposals to prospective customers, we outlined **step-by-step** exactly what we'd do for their business. We didn't hold anything back; we detailed what tools we'd use, what we'd use to measure results, what action steps we'd take, and what our strategy would be. In fact, our proposals were so detailed that our prospects could easily turn around and just implement it by themselves. **But they didn't,** and we knew they wouldn't, because doing search engine optimization wasn't their forte. We knew that in the end, they'd turn to us to implement, so we didn't fear giving away the proverbial farm.

We may have lost *some* clients by being so detailed, and we may have given other SEO companies an advantage by giving our entire strategy and plan away for free during the proposal stage, but that's fine... we always had an abundance mindset, and if we lost a few clients then that didn't bother us because we always knew there were thousands more for us to chase.

Leading with value is without a doubt the single best piece of advice that I can give new entrepreneurs as they begin to build their first successful business.

My current business is based 100% around leading with value. In fact, I often get asked "how the heck do you make any money?"

I love that question. Every time I'm asked that question it means that people see how much value I give away for free. In fact, most people don't even *know* how to work with me, because I don't typically have any outward-facing sales pages, and I *never* ask people to become my customers. Instead, I lead with value, and I know that the right prospects will end up asking me about my paid programs, or they'll trigger certain actions within my CRM (customer relationship management) tool that will send them the opportunity to enroll in one of my paid programs or courses.

Because I lead with value, I no longer need to convince anyone to work with me. I do not accept offers for one-on-one client work anymore, and I get to do what I want when I want. All because I lead with value. I give so much away for free in the form of ebooks, webinars, video courses, and other resources that **people come to me** and people want to pay me for my programs and courses. See how different that is from *convincing* and begging people to work with you?

Figure out a way that you can lead with value, and your business will have a much greater chance at succeeding.

Have a Multi-Tiered Product Mix

For one reason or another, most business schools and business books don't teach you this one **extremely important** strategy: you need to have a multi-tiered product mix. In less fancy business terms, your business needs to have solutions, products, or services at different pricing points, rather than just a high-end solution or a low-end solution.

Most big businesses know exactly where they fit in the marketplace. Rolex, for example, know that they play in the high-end watch marketplace, with their watches costing $10,000 and up. Swatch, on the other hand, makes much more affordable watches (starting at less than $100!), so they clearly play in the lower end of the market.

Both approaches can be successful, and indeed, both companies I've used as examples are successful.

But... having a multi-tiered product mix, or products at *different* price points, can bring far greater rewards.

Just ask Apple. For years the iPhone was the most expensive and sought-after smartphone on the market, signifying the top end of the market. It seemed like every upper-middle class American had an iPhone, whereas the lower end of the market was flooded with Blackberry devices and entry-level Android devices. Just like with their extremely pricy MacBooks and iMacs, Apple was okay with pricing themselves out of the mass market.

In 2013 the tech giants from California surprised everybody by announcing the iPhone 5c. The 5c was priced at $99 for subsidized phone contracts in the United States, making it the most affordable iPhone ever. This was a huge jump into the lower end of the smartphone market, and it paid huge dividends for Tim Cook and Apple. The iPhone 5c went on to become one of the company's bestselling phones of all time. The full-price and fully-featured iPhone 5, meanwhile, also shattered sales records, proving that by rolling out a multi-tiered product mix, Apple still didn't cannibalize their sales... they simply reached new customers that they wouldn't have otherwise reached due to price.

Now, Apple plays in all tiers of the market. They have lower-priced offerings for MacBooks, they have different tiers of pricing for iPads, and multiple tiers of pricing for the Apple Watch. Best of all, this doesn't necessarily mean the market is flooded with their lowest-priced offerings. On the contrary, sales of **all** tiers continue to flourish, making Apple the most valuable company in the world.

So what does this have to do with your business? By all means, I'm not suggesting that you have to cater to all different segments of the market like Apple does. But, this should illustrate the power of having multiple tiers of product offerings; they open up options and lower the barrier of becoming a customer.

When I was running NewGen Consultants, our core offer was our monthly search engine optimization package. This package ranged from $1,000 per month all the way up to $5,000 per month depending on the company size and industry size. We had many sales conversations, and closed people into our smaller packages at a decent rate, but my business partner and I knew that if we could get people to just work with us once, they'd see how good we were and would want to buy into our higher-tiered packages.

And thus, our multi-tiered product mix was born. We realized that if we could find an offer that was more affordable to begin our working relationship with clients, then once we massively over-delivered and got them results they'd want more.

Rather than trying to sell people directly into our monthly subscription service, we decided to try to sell them a $500 SEO (Search Engine Optimization) audit. Our SEO audit was a comprehensive one-time service where we crawled their entire website and came up with step by step improvements that they should implement to get more website traffic, and thus get more customers and clients from the internet.

These SEO audits took a few hours for us to

complete, but they were well worth it as they opened the door for us to new clients. People were less hesitant to purchase it as it was relatively inexpensive, and we knew that it put us in a position of trust with them. They were trusting us to give them actionable suggestions for their website, so when it came time for them to implement those suggestions we knew they'd turn to us.

The result of this was that we sold our first SEO audit at the end of one of our free seminars, and that resulted in us sitting at the table with the CEO of a multi-million dollar corporation a few weeks later to present our findings. It's crazy to think that just a few months earlier we were wondering how the heck newer marketing agencies could "get in" with larger corporations with deep pockets, and we accomplished that feat just by offering solutions at different price points!

I was taught to look at the "multi-tiered product mix" as a bullseye. Picture a bullseye made up of many concentric circles. Each ring of the bullseye represents another service or product within your multi-tiered product mix. The center – the bullseye – is your core offer, or your highest-priced offer. For some businesses this offer will be $10,000, while for some it could be $100… it completely depends on your unique business.

The outer-most ring is your least expensive offer. For some businesses this might be $7, or in the case of my marketing agency, the outer ring was $500 for the SEO audit. Depending on your business and your offerings, you'll have a different number of rings that lead to your bullseye, but the important thing is to plot out your rings so that you know the path that leads to the bullseye.

In the case of NewGen Consultants, the outer ring was our SEO audit for $500. Just inside that was our on-page search engine optimization package, which was a one-time fee of $2,000. Inside of that was our complete website redesign package, which ranged anywhere from $2,000 to $8,000 (as time went on, we increased our prices). The center of our bullseye was our monthly packages, which ranged from $1,000 per month to $5,000 per month.

In the case of my business today, I have even more rings since I have more and more solutions for the people that I serve. I always have very low-ticket solutions that help me build relationships with my customers and build up trust. My low-ticket solutions range from $7 to $97, and in each of those I make sure to deliver at least 10 times the value of what I charge. Then, I have mid-tier offers ranging from $297 to $497, and just inside of those I have a series of programs and courses that sell for $997. Finally, at the center of my bullseye today is my flagship $1,997 program called **The Ultimate Profit Model,** but over time I know that I'm going to need to further build out my bullseye of offerings so that I can work with the segment of my customers that want even more from me. I could easily introduce $10,000 personalized one-on-one packages, or even live events. Over time my multi-tiered product mix will change, but it's essential that you plan yours out today.

I've talked in-depth about the importance of having a more affordable option to lead people to your higher-ticket items, but let's talk about the reverse. So many newpreneurs believe that they can enter markets with an extremely low price point and make up for it through volume. First of all, doing this results in a **lot** of extra work, and in many cases simply leads to a revenue ceiling.

In my current market, a lot of newpreneurs flood the marketplace with $7 ebooks and think that they will make good money. Think about the work that goes in to making $100,000 off a $7 ebook… you'd need to make 14,285 sales at that price point just to make six-figures in a year. It's possible, for sure, and it's been done before, but it's certainly not the smartest path to replacing your full-time income.

Instead, consider selling something for $500. At that price point, you only need **200 people** to say yes and pull out their credit card in order for you to make six-figures in a year. That's just four customers per week. Increase the price to $2,000, and basic math reveals that you only need **50 sales** to make six-figures, or just one sale per week. See how much more manageable that is?

No matter what your business is, make sure you take the time to draw out your multi-tiered product mix. You can see these in action in **any** successful business, online or offline. Dentists love when you come in for cleanings because that's their outer ring of their multi-tiered product mix bullseye. When you come in for a cleaning, they find cavities. Filling cavities brings them even more profit. From there, they recommend braces. From there, you need a root canal over time. They lead you along their multi-tiered product mix (based on your needs, of course), but they don't put all their eggs in one basket. Imagine a dentist that only did cleanings… they *could* make money, but it'll never be as much money as if they offered many different tiers of services.

While we're on the topic of pricing, as an entrepreneur now (whether you feel like one or not, you are an entrepreneur!), you need to understand that **you no longer get paid for your time.** Entrepreneurs get paid for their impact. **Money is not a measure of time; it's a measure of value.**

Read that again.

Money is not a measure of time. It's a measure of value.

As an entrepreneur, you need to get out of the employee mindset. Rather than charging clients for your time, you need to get into the mindset of charging them for your impact and for your value. When my business partner and I made websites for clients, our very first website deal was for a measly $1,000. We were over the moon about it, though! Why? Because we knew it was a very basic website and it would only take us about five hours to make. That works out to $200 per hour, or $100 per hour each!

The thing is, the business we made that website for would go on to make *way more* than $1,000 from their website. That website was worth far more than $1,000 to them, but we weren't thinking about it in those terms.

Fast forward a year later, and we were a year older and wiser. On the way to a meeting with a multi-million dollar manufacturing firm, my business partner and I were discussing what price we'd name for a basic website, which we estimated would take us two weeks to complete.

"Let's say something crazy like $6,000!" we excitedly said during the car ride. It would be the highest price we had ever charged for a website, but we were feeling good because we knew the company had deep pockets.

Our presentation to their team went really well, and although we typically didn't talk price at the end of our presentations (we used to take the time to do our due diligence and send a proposal), the company said that they wanted to work with us, and asked us to name a price.

I'll never forget what happened next.

"Six thousand dollars," I confidently said to the room full of people, including one of the company's vice presidents.

A second of silence went by, and I was beginning to think that we had blown the deal by asking for too much money, but then the whole room burst out into laughter.

"Haha, hey Joe – you can just put that on your corporate card!" one of them joked.

I didn't know whether to feel humiliated or not. After

all, I just received confirmation that I would make $3,000 for my half of the deal.

When we had time to go home and digest everything that happened, my business partner and I both knew that we could have charged them for more. Luckily, after they laughed and joked about putting the small expense on their corporate card, I kept the door open by indicating that if their budget allowed for further upgrades, we could also perform search engine optimization on their website.

In the end, we didn't want to move the goalposts too much on them after naming our initial price, so we ended up closing the deal for $8,000. Realistically, we could have gotten at least $10,000 from them for the website (if not more!), but that served as an important business lesson. When you're an entrepreneur, your services are worth **a lot** to your clients. Even if the company paid $20,000 for the website, it would likely bring them in at least $100,000 of revenue within that calendar year, so it would be well worth it for them.

Make sure you always remember that you don't get paid – and you don't charge – for your time. You get paid, and you charge for, your impact and the results that you bring.

What said that the website we made for them was only worth $8,000? Because we felt that's what our *time* was worth? In fact, they weren't buying our *time*, they were buying a *website*, which was worth far more to them than our time.

Every Customer is a Person

The last bit of "business advice" that I want to include is that it's essential to remember that every customer is a person. Even if your business is a B2B company (business to business, meaning your company sells to other businesses rather than to end consumers), you need to remember that no sale occurs without another human on the other side. (At the time of writing, computers still don't have credit cards and bank accounts, so they can't buy stuff without a human saying "yes")

Especially when you sell things online, it's easy to forget that there's a real, live person on the other side of the computer.

When I started selling online programs at the end of 2013, I needed to remind myself of that fact more than ever. In most cases, I don't ever even talk to my customers or email them… they just go through my automated sales and marketing funnels and buy my products. It's great for me, but it's dangerous if I don't remember to incorporate an incredible customer experience into things.

Because I'm cognizant of this fact, I spend time each week going through and reviewing all of my customers to see what special experience I can do for them. At the time of writing this, last week I mailed a customer in Illinois a gift card to a local movie theater and included a hand-written note telling him to take his daughter to a movie some time. I learned that he has a 10-year-old daughter from his Facebook (creepy, right!?), and knew that he'd love the small touch. It cost me $20 to build a special experience for a customer who has spent thousands of dollars on my products. Is that worth it? I'd say so.

Aside from doing little things like that, the human element should be baked into all of your business' processes. As an entrepreneur, you need to map out your entire process – from the initial contact with the potential customer to the sales pitch to the proposal stage (if you have one) to the closing of the sale to the delivery of the sale (whether you have a product or a service). At each step of the process that the customer experiences, how can you optimize their experience?

How can you make the proposal stage more enjoyable? In my own business, I always used to include funny videos greeting them to their proposals, so they'd open the proposal up and see a funny video of my business partner and I in front of a green screen. It added a little bit of a human element, and we got more praise for that than most other things we did.

How can you make the delivery of the sale more enjoyable? Companies like HostGator do a fantastic job of this by having a quick-start guide for new customers. When you sign up for HostGator's web hosting services, it's overwhelming to maneuver around their control panel and to try to figure out what your first steps are (there's your domain name, your email accounts, your web hosting, anti-virus services, etc.!).

Once you sign-up, though, you're directed to a very clear page outlining step by step what you should do. They take a very confusing and overwhelming process and make it simple... just follow the steps. I recently underwent this process with them, and it was the least stressful experience I've had with a web host. Somewhere within the organization someone thought about the customer, and realized that upon logging in for the first time they had the opportunity to control their experience and make it positive by putting such a helpful resource together.

Contrast that with my recent experience with a product that I use to give me WiFi on the go. I purchased the product, and at the time of purchase was told that it would take two weeks to ship. I understood that going into it, and was happy to wait the two weeks.

Two weeks later, though, and I was still in the dark. Had the product shipped? When could I expect it? Their website didn't give me any additional information, so I opened a support ticket with them. They told me that I would receive an email confirmation when the product shipped, but that was the first time I was informed of that.

They may have understood the process on their end (customer orders, and then upon shipment the customer would receive an email), but no one in the business thought about the process that the customer goes through. No one thought about what the *customer* is doing, thinking, and wondering during the time between ordering the product and the product shipping. Had they included information on their website about my order, or had they sent one email per week saying "Hey Brian! Unfortunately your order hasn't shipped yet, but we wanted to keep you in the loop. We're working hard to get more supplies in" then I would have been far more understanding. Plus, it would have saved them time and money as I wouldn't have had to open a support ticket.

Plot out your business processes and your workflow not only from your perspective, but also through the customer's lens. Figure out what their experience is like at each step of the way, and make it as remarkable as possible.

Above all else, remember that business doesn't have to be complicated. Deliver something that people want, and always remember that every customer is a human. Make their experiences as positive as possible and you'll have happy customers that keep buying from you and that share your solution with the world.

Business isn't hard. You don't need a business plan, and you don't need to use crazy complicated technology or strategies. Give people what they want.

If you're looking for some golden nugget of wisdom that will give you your breakthrough, or if you think there's some *secret* to succeeding as an entrepreneur, then stop looking. What are you waiting for? Just start.

9

Enjoy the Journey

Above all else, being an entrepreneur is about enjoying the journey. As you start your business, you're about to embark on the most exciting, the most frustrating, the scariest, the happiest, and the most rewarding journey of your life.

That famous Steve Jobs quote from one of Apple's most famous commercials ever always makes me smile when I think about what it means to be an entrepreneur.

"Here's to the crazy ones, the misfits, the rebels, the troublemakers, the round pegs in the square holes... the ones who see things differently - they're not fond of rules... You can quote them, disagree with them, glorify or vilify them, but the only thing you can't do is ignore them because they change things... they push the human race forward, and while some may see them as the crazy ones, we see genius, because the ones who are crazy enough to think that they can change the world, are the ones who do," said the late Apple CEO in a 1997 commercial.

I love that quote because Jobs points out that you have to be crazy enough to think that you can change the world, to change *your* world. Being an entrepreneur is about going outside of your comfort zone.

Now let me talk about failure, because ultimately that's the scariest part about being an entrepreneur. As many successes as I've had in my entrepreneurial life, I've had many failures. My biggest "failure" of all came in the latter half of 2013, and it was that one failure that ultimately pushed me into the life that I've always dreamed of.

You've read about my marketing agency, NewGen Consultants, throughout this book, but up to this point I haven't addressed why I no longer run that business. After all, the business was flourishing, we grew to six-figures in revenue really quickly, and we had happy clients all across the United States.

But... the business wasn't balanced. My business partner and I were working 80 hours per week, and we were dealing with clients that weren't always fun to work with. I remember spending Christmas Eve at the office of one of our clients fixing their email server while my family laughed and dined, and I remember pulling all-nighters to fix websites that had crashed because of a client trying to install a plugin or a script on their own.

In other words, NewGen was my life. And my business partner's. And I could see that he was getting burned out, and deep down I knew that I was getting burned out and I wasn't having fun with it anymore.

Every entrepreneur's worst dream is to see their company shut down, and on September 23rd, 2013 I experienced what I considered to be my biggest failure as an entrepreneur. As I was sitting down to eat lunch, I received an email from my business partner explaining that he was done and wanted to wind the business down.

Boom – that hurt.

Here's a business that I spent almost two years of my life working on. Here's a business that I spent 80 hours a week on, and a business that was one of my proudest accomplishments as we grew it to six-figures in revenue so quickly, starting from scratch, and with a business partner who had zero experience in the industry before we started working together.

I'll never forget that day. I remember reading the email and then looking up from my phone at the room around me. I remember looking at the walls, at the ceiling, at the table, at the chairs.

And in that moment, what I realized was that nothing was falling. The ceiling wasn't coming down on me, the chairs weren't crumbling, and the world went on. For months I knew that the day would come as I could see my business partner getting burned out, but I still felt like it would be the worst day of my life. I felt like the sky would come falling down.

But it didn't. And in that very moment, I realized that failure isn't all that bad. All of the horrible things that you think would happen don't. In fact, it's a pretty peaceful moment. Every door in the world opens up in that moment, rather than having one door close. That moment made me fearless; if that was failure, and failure was as bad as it could get, then bring it on!

So why do I tell you this story? For three reasons.

First, failure isn't so bad. I won't beat this point too hard because my story above illustrates it, and chances are you won't fully embrace this point until you experience it yourself. But trust me – it's not as bad as you think.

Second, failure can teach us our most important lessons, so it's time to *embrace failure*, not be afraid of it. I learned more about myself and about business in my two years as CEO of NewGen Consultants than I learned in my entire life – including my four years at one of the top business universities in the United States.

Thanks to the failure of my marketing agency, I began to understand how successful (and unsuccessful) businesses operate. With that knowledge, I was able to launch my next (and current) venture, where I work with entrepreneurs, wantrepreneurs, and solopreneurs from all around the world to launch, build, and automate their businesses. My business now is completely scalable, and it allows me to do the things that I enjoy most when it comes to being an entrepreneur.

Had I not "failed" with NewGen, I would have never learned about the importance of building a *scalable* business. I would have never even considered *scalability* as much as I do now. In fact, because of the experience of failure due to a business that wasn't very scalable, I immediately say **NO** to any and all opportunities that I can identify as not scalable.

And finally, I tell you this story because after that happened, I became obsessed with figuring out how to build a business that will create a genuinely **good life**. This obsession led me to attend **Camp Good Life Project** in 2014, where Jonathan Fields, the founder of the Good Life Project, organized over 200 entrepreneurs and world-changers to spend nearly a week together at a camp site in upstate New York.

There, Jonathan introduced all of us to what he calls the "three buckets of a Good Life." Jonathan argues that the quality of your life is determined by three "buckets:" your **contribution** bucket, your **connection** bucket, and your **vitality** bucket. According to Jonathan, your overall life quality is actually determined by your *least filled* bucket. In other words, if your contribution bucket and your connection buckets are filled to the brim, but your vitality bucket is empty, then you won't have a truly good life.

So what are these buckets? The names somewhat give them away, but I'll give you a brief overview into them. Your contribution bucket is made up of everything that you *contribute* to the world, such as your work, your community service, the content that you create, if you coach a youth soccer team, etc. To fill this bucket, do things that contribute to the world around you.

The connection bucket is all about connecting with other people. Filling this bucket is possible by having conversations with friends, family, acquaintances, or even strangers. Connecting with yourself and nature also fills the connection bucket.

The third and final bucket, vitality, is about doing things that make you feel alive. To fill this bucket, you can sleep well, exercise, meditate, or eat well. These are all things that make you feel good.

So why do I tell you these things? Because Jonathan's view of a good life is especially important for entrepreneurs. It's so easy to get wrapped up in your business, and let that consume your life. But as I've learned first-hand, if you're not consistently filling *all three* of your buckets, you ultimately won't be as happy as you can be, regardless of how successful your business gets.

An entrepreneur whose contribution and connection buckets are overflowing won't be completely satisfied with his or her life if his/her vitality bucket is empty.

When you find yourself stuck in a rut or not feeling positive about your life, it's time to double down on whichever bucket is running dry. As an entrepreneur, you have the benefit of making your own schedule and focusing your energies wherever you want to. As someone who primarily does business online, I sometimes feel like my connection bucket is running dry since I don't have an office to go to and I don't necessarily see people every day.

To fix that, I have a lot of options. For this reason, I often work from coffee shops, and usually find myself getting into intriguing conversations with my fellow coffee shop visitors. Or, I hop on a Skype video call with someone in my network to see how they're doing and to just talk about life. Or, thanks to modern technology, it's possible to hop online to services such as blab.im and talk to people from all over the world about pretty much any topic you can think of.

As I get more experienced and as my business gets

more automated and streamlined, I am becoming better at structuring my weeks around these three buckets. Every week I have activities carved out that fill all three of my buckets; I make sure to exercise each week, I make sure to connect with my friends and family, and I make sure to create things that positively contribute to the world.

Of course, you'll have times where you're so consumed with your business that other things will slip, and that's okay. But if you find yourself going a year with minimal sleep, then eventually that's going to catch up. By all means, though, I'm not saying don't hustle... on the contrary, I love what I do, so you can often find me working 12+ hour days. When I first started Premiership Talk, I would regularly get around four hours of sleep per night (I would stay up all night writing new blog posts since English news breaks in the United States around 3am EST). That's okay (and fun!) for a time, but keeping the other buckets in mind will undoubtedly contribute to your happiness, and your happiness has a direct impact on your business's bottom line.

Everything is Your Responsibility

Perhaps the most rewarding part of being an entrepreneur is that everything is your responsibility. As an employee, you don't need to worry about marketing, you don't need to worry about human resources, you don't need to worry about creating corporate culture, you don't need to worry about sales, you don't need to worry about customer satisfaction, and you don't need to worry about customer service. Unless, of course, you work in any *one* of those areas, but unless you're the CEO then you don't care about *all* of those areas.

As an entrepreneur, though, it all rests on you. I *love* the fact that **everything** in my business is my responsibility. It takes a while to get used to that, but once you accept that fact, it can separate you from the rest of the world.

What does this mean? At its most basic level, you are now responsible for how much money you're going to make. You are directly responsible for what you do on a daily basis. And, you are directly responsible for who you work with and what happens in your life. Even the things that *feel* like they're not your responsibility *are* your responsibility as a business owner. For example, when a client's website crashed due to an error by the web host, I knew that it wasn't "my fault." But, in the eyes of the client, my company was responsible for their website's uptime.

Because I always had the mindset that *everything* is our responsibility – the good **and** the bad – I always happily took the blame. By doing so, I've always been able to come up with on-the-fly solutions to pretty much any problem. Rather than saying to the client, "sorry, this was the web host's fault," I was able to point their website to a backup directory where I had cloned their website. In the eyes of the client, I held myself responsible for *everything*, even the things that were seemingly out of my control. Can you imagine how much faith clients had in me and my business?

If you're not making the money that you want to make, that's your fault. If you make more money than you dreamed of, that's your fault too. The good things, the bad things, they're all your fault.

When you accept that, you immediately become your own best resource. Way too many new entrepreneurs have the tendency to rely on help from outside forces and from outside people. With the resources available at our fingertips today, there's no reason to rely on someone else for your success. Remember – *your* success is *your* responsibility.

I've never been allowed myself to get held back by my own lack of knowledge. When I started Premiership Talk, I had no clue how to create a website... so I spent hours on

Google and YouTube learning how to do exactly that. When I saw that bigger, more successful websites had fancy "ad servers" displaying their advertising campaigns, I Googled "free ad server self install" and taught myself how to do that.

And before you think it, I promise you that I'm no different than you are. I've just accepted the fact that I alone am responsible for all of my successes and failures, and because of that I have become my own best resource. Part of the journey is that you need to understand that you're your own best resource, and have confidence and peace with that fact. When you realize that all you need is you, and you're confident that you can resolve *any* challenge that you're faced with, then you'll feel powerful and at peace with the journey.

You've Got Choices

On top of everything being your responsibility, another universal truth is that **you've got choices**, especially as an entrepreneur. When I hear people talk about how much they hate their jobs, I always chuckle. My first question to them is "why do you go to work every day then?"

People have the tendency to say "because I have to."

In fact, you don't. No one *has to* do anything. If you wanted to, you could sit on your couch and watch TV in your pajamas every day for the next year. But you won't, because you have bills to pay, things to do, and because it would be quite unhealthy. So, you're *choosing* to go to work, so that you can make money and pay for these things that you want.

The same concept is truer than ever for entrepreneurs. People will tell you that there are things that you "have to" do as an entrepreneur. You "have to" go to networking events. You "have to" say yes to everything (that one cracks me up). You "have to" work Monday through Friday because that's what everyone else does. You "have to" have a website. You "have to" have business cards. You "have to" respond to emails the same day.

You don't.

Trust me, you don't.

You have the power to choose anything that you want in life and in your business. Now, you can't be erratic and all over the place, and you should always strive to make the best customer experience possible, but outside of that you have the power to choose what you do.

At the tail end of 2013 I made the decision to stop working with clients. Everyone told me that you need to work one-on-one with clients, but I fully committed to creating and launching online programs, and I now have over 3,000 students from around the world. I don't personally enjoy client-based work, so I don't do it anymore. It's as simple as that. On the rare occasions where I *do* take one-on-one clients, it's on my terms, it's for exorbitant fees, and it's only with people who I absolutely want to work with.

Because I no longer rely on picking up clients, I no longer have business cards, my website was down for three months in 2015 after getting hacked, and when I go to networking events it's just to have fun. These are all decisions that I've consciously made, despite the fact that traditional business advice says I "have to" do those things.

You've also read about my first major company, Premiership Talk, throughout this book. I no longer actively run or manage the website, because I choose not to. After 5,604 posts, tens of thousands of comments from readers, millions of visits from readers from over 200 countries around the world, after managing 53 writers over the years, and after generating more advertising revenue than I ever thought possible with a website that I started just for fun, I chose to not do it anymore. Why? Because it wasn't enjoyable for me anymore. I *love* being a fan, but I fell out of love with having to write articles each and every day, manage advertising deals, and manage my writers. And as an entrepreneur, that's my prerogative.

But what about all the things you *do* want to do? You can choose those things too. You can choose to go bowling every Friday if you want. Or go for a walk in the middle of the day. Or sleep until 9am. Or walk out of a restaurant because you don't like their menu.

The important thing here is that **your choices will define your future.** Your choices will define everything about you, your life, and your business. So make those choices consciously. Don't outsource your choices to society's expectations of you.

At the end of the day, your journey is made up of hundreds of thousands of choices. You can make the choice to blame other people for why you can't succeed, or you can make the choice to ignore all the reasons why you think you *can't* do something, and just choose to succeed. You can make the choice to blame outside circumstances (I'm too old, I'm too young, I'm too dumb, I don't know the right people), or you can choose to succeed.

My challenge to you is to choose to succeed. Forget everything else, and have the dogged determination that you need to succeed. All you need is you, and luckily for you, you've got you. You don't need anything or anyone else.

When you do all of this, you'll have ups... and you'll have downs. Enjoy every part of the journey. Most people want to be their own boss and become an entrepreneur, but luckily for you and I, 99% of them will never put the work in to actually make it happen. They *wish* they were entrepreneurs, and one day they'll look back and regret never taking action.

You're in a position that most people will never get to enjoy. Relish that. The "cost" of this opportunity is that you'll have challenges, you'll have downs where you feel like quitting, and you'll have days where it feels like nothing is going right. Those obstacles are there to separate the successful people from the unsuccessful ones. It's so easy to quit when these challenges arise... and that's why most people never succeed.

My challenge to you is to *choose to succeed*. Make the very conscious decision today – and every day – that you are going to succeed. Don't let anything or anyone get in the way of that. Enjoy the journey, embrace the failures, celebrate the successes, and you'll be an unstoppable force.

If you do all of these things, then you'll be a truly successful entrepreneur. I know you can.

Afterword

This book is a culmination of my nine years of "being an entrepreneur." When I talk to people about "being an entrepreneur," I always realize that it's not something that happens overnight. Instead, *all* of us are born as entrepreneurs... most people just choose to give up that status by playing it safe, by living by society's expectations, and by forgetting that we have the power to choose.

The most important lessons that I've learned as an entrepreneur are all contained within this book. When I was 18 and deciding which college I wanted to attend, I made the decision to attend one of the top business universities in the United States. There, I imagined that I would learn the essentials of starting my own business, but instead I learned from textbooks filled with knowledge from the decades prior. Most of these lessons revolved around the "old way" of doing business... including making business plans, deciding which radio stations to advertise on, and how to analyze the "competition."

Of course, these things are no longer as relevant in today's world, where social media, the internet, and key differentiators are far more important.

Regardless, my four years at school were where I learned the most about "being an entrepreneur." Why? Because I did it. I didn't wait for anyone's permission, and I didn't wait for the perfect moment. *Tip: the perfect moment, or the perfect time, doesn't really exist.*

While I've revealed many of my most important lessons from the past decade, at the end of the day I hope that you take one very important lesson home: *nothing* that anyone else tells you is necessarily going to be true for you, and you have the ability, the power, and the knowledge to discover your own truths, if only you commit and decide to succeed.

The best way to become a better driver is to drive, not to sit at home and read about driving. The best way to become a better soccer player is to get out there and kick the ball around, regardless of your level of expertise. The best way to become a better painter is to paint. Sure, there is an endless amount of wisdom written in books and across the internet, but at the end of the day the most important thing is to *do it*.

The sooner you realize that there's no golden nugget of information, the sooner you can begin your journey of self-exploration and self-learning. After all, there's no better way to learn... and there's no better time to *start* than now.

At the end of the day, there's no advice more relevant than these three things:

1) Start now... there's no time like the present, and waiting won't accomplish anything or make you any more prepared

2) Embrace failure... failure isn't the opposite of success, it's a part of success. Failure isn't all that bad, and will make you fearless.

3) Take action... it's the *only way* to change your future. Fortune favors the action-takers.

If you're wondering what to do now that you've read this entire book, all I ask is that you go out and **do it**. Start your business, celebrate your successes, learn from your failures, and don't let *anybody* **ever** tell you that it can't be done.

Indeed, you can accomplish anything. As long as you decide, commit, and relentlessly take action. The world is yours.

Bonus Chapter:
Advice from my Tribe

Upon completion of this book, I took a massive deep breath and looked back on the entire project with a deep sense of pride and accomplishment. What I quickly realized, though, is that the lessons, learnings, and adventures that I shared with you throughout these pages wouldn't have been possible without what I like to think of as my "tribe."

As an entrepreneur, you will inevitably find some like-minded people who "get you." These are the people who understand your struggles, celebrate your successes, and always are willing to lend an open ear (and open arms) to you at any point in your journey. They're also the ones who you can turn to for advice, as they're always willing to share their own experiences, triumphs, and tribulations.

It only felt right to include some words of wisdom from my various fellow entrepreneurs from two of my tribes: my Camp Good Life Project tribe, who I attend summer camp with in upstate New York and learn from some of the world's most accomplished speakers and entrepreneurs, and my Awesomeness Fest tribe, who are – suitably named – the most **awesome** people that I know, as several hundred of us travel to exotic locations around the world twice a year to learn, celebrate, and connect at an incredibly deep level.

Without further ado, following are the words of wisdom that my various tribe members gave when I asked them what their best advice is for newpreneurs as they begin their journey of becoming an entrepreneur…

"You can't judge a fish by how well it can climb a tree. Just because you're not good at one particular thing, no matter how much weight society puts on that thing, doesn't mean you're worthless; it just means that your calling is somewhere else. Chase your calling until you find it, or it finds you." – **Justin Traub, motivategen.com**

"Your comfort zone is not the goal. It's only a resting place between periods of growth." – **Dawn DelVecchio, dawndelvecchio.com**

"Imagine you had a magic wand, you can wish for anything to be true in three years. You can have one thing, solve one problem, be doing one thing and around one type of person. The answers will define your path of exactly what you should be doing. So long as you want those things you will be on the right path." – **Iain Grae, saraceway.com**

"Moving from wantrepreneur to entrepreneur can feel like a head versus heart decision. The perceived security of being an employee versus taking that risk and following your passion is often the wrestle. Identify and apply your strengths, collaborate with others to use their strengths for your self-belief and success." – **Murray Guest, inspiremybusiness.com**

"Welcome failure with both arms. You will be alone. You will face defeat several times. And you will feel like s***. This is what you signed up for. But I can assure you that these healthy dosages of dejection will be sprinkled with rare instances of elation and they will more than make it worth it. Here's another trick I learnt - when you face failure, share it with 10 people you look up to. You will probably find an opportunity in one of those conversations. Most of our innovations in our service delivery came while narrating horror stories to our friends and people we look towards for advice. That's when the best ideas happened. Not when I shared our success stories." – **Manu Dhawan, spaceworxindia.com**

"Learn to balance advice from others with your own intuition and originality. Be bold." – **Cynthia Morris, originalimpulse.com**

And finally, my dear friend and incredibly inspiring entrepreneur, **Gordy Bal, of ctr.com**, wanted me to share the "3 Realizations of Conscious Entrepreneurship". Here's Gordy's text, in full:

3 Realizations of Conscious Entrepreneurship

1. Get Uncomfortable

It is easy to become complacent and mediocre. The problem is that when we operate like this, we are signaling our minds and bodies that we no longer need them. If we are not growing and expanding, then we are dying. We must observe the areas in our lives where opportunities for expansion arise and seize them as they are the portals to access our higher selves.

How do we do this? Wake up in the morning and ask yourself, what can I do today that I would normally put off or avoid doing because it would make me uncomfortable? Start every day by making this decision and then DO IT. It can be as simple as calling your mother or father to tell them you love them, or as crazy as making dinner for a homeless person. Start with something super simple and let it compound each day. Not only does this empower you. but it empowers those around you.

2. Be Part of a BOLD Mission

The world is changing, and it is changing faster than ever. The exponential growth of technology is showing glimpses of a not-so-distant future that could only have been conceived of in sci-fi movies a few decades ago. So many old paradigms in business are shifting at an accelerated rate. Uber with transportation, Tesla with energy, Bitcoin with finance are just a few examples. What aligns with your aspirations and ambitions? Find a mission that is **BOLD** and dive in with both feet - or better yet, set your intention and let the mission find you.

Making a HUGE impact is no longer just a pipe dream. Technology, connectedness, freeflow of information are all showing how everything is truly possible. Set an intention of what you want to do in the world which is so big that when you share it with others they look at you and think you are partially insane! You'll be surprised at how many other people want to do crazy stuff around you but are just too afraid to admit it or step outside of their comfort zone. Make a bold declaration: own it, live it, breathe it, act it. You will begin to notice people and events occurring around you that will begin to materialize this intention.

3. Be a Source of Utility to the World

Traditional enterprises have been mostly focused on profit first. It has been about extrapolating as much value from the planet as possible and giving it back to the shareholders. This is not groundbreaking news by any means, however it still deserves some attention to make a clear distinction. This way of business has served its purpose and has helped millions and millions of people have jobs, birthed innovation, and progressed society as a whole. The problem is that this model no longer serves humanity. As profits soared, the people and the planet have suffered.

Instead of focusing on profit first, focus on solving a problem that is in need of innovation. What do you see on a daily basis that is negatively impacting the planet that you know can be improved through innovation? Prove the solution on a small scale in your community first and then see how this can be scaled to other parts of the world. By alleviating suffering for the planet or people through innovation, profit will follow because you are focused on providing value and utility to the world. The beauty of this kind of profit is that it comes with a much more liberated energy field or karmic score.